THE 100+ SERIES™

Reproducible Activities

Building Writing Skills

Laying the Foundation for Written Expression

By
Kelly Speer Hatfield

Cover Design by
Matthew Van Zomeren

Inside Illustrations by
Tim Foley

Published by Instructional Fair
an imprint of

Frank Schaffer Publications®

Instructional Fair

Frank Schaffer Publications®

Instructional Fair is an imprint of Frank Schaffer Publications.

Printed in the United States of America. All rights reserved. Limited Reproduction Permission: Permission to duplicate these materials is limited to the person for whom they are purchased. Reproduction for an entire school or school district is unlawful and strictly prohibited. Frank Schaffer Publications is an imprint of School Specialty Publishing. Copyright © 2002 School Specialty Publishing.

Send all inquiries to:
Frank Schaffer Publications
8720 Orion Place
Columbus, Ohio 43240-2111

Building Writing Skills—Grades 2-3

ISBN 0-7424-0222-3

3 4 5 6 7 8 9 10 QPD 12 11 10 09

Table of Contents

Under the Sea (identifying complete sentences) 4
Itty Bitty Bugs (identifying types of sentences) 5
The Hike (capitals and end marks) 6
A Trip to the Zoo (identifying complete sentences) 7
It's a Puzzle! (word order) 8
Peanut Butter and Jelly (subjects and predicates) 9
The Toy Store (subjects) 10
Toys, Toys, Toys (predicates) 11
Once Upon a Time (subjects and predicates) 12
Wild Wolves (subjects and predicates) 13
The Fire (nouns and pronouns) 14
Lights, Camera, Action! (action verbs) 15
Quiet, Please! (nonaction verbs) 16
How Does Your Garden Grow? (subject/verb agreement) 17
Going Up! (present tense—to be) 18
Ed, Ted, and Fred (past-tense regular verbs) 19
Look Before You Leap (past-tense irregular verbs) 20
Monkey Business (past tense—to be) 21
The Turtle's Trip (past-tense subject/verb agreement) 22
This and That (compound subjects) 23
Read and Write (compound predicates) 24
A Birthday Party (compound sentences) 25
A Winter's Day (compound sentences) 26
The Best Day Ever (run-on sentences) 27
All Tied Up (stringy sentences) 28
Eli Is Excited! (stringy sentences) 29
Packing a Suitcase (commas in a series) 30
Adjective Art (adding adjectives) 31
Oh, Say, Can You See? (adding adjectives) 32
The Case of the Missing Grapes (how and when) 33
Hide and Seek (where) 34
Save the Day (vivid verbs) 35
Just Because (cause and effect) 36
Super Sentences! (the 5Ws + how) 37
Under Construction (building sentences) 38
Ready, Set, Morph! (complex sentences) 39
What's the Big Idea? (paragraphs) 40
Field Day (extraneous details) 41
Animal Addresses (indentation) 42
Topics in the Tropics (topic sentences) 43
Up, Up, and Away (topic sentences) 44
Lean on a Friend (supporting sentences) 45
Perfect Pizza (examples) 46
Build a Bridge (transitions) 47
In the Kitchen (sequencing) 48
Great Endings (concluding sentences) 49
End of the Day (concluding sentences) 50
Horsing Around (expository paragraphs) 51
Sssssssssnakes! (informative paragraphs) 52
Stripes or Spots? (descriptive paragraphs) 53
How Do You Do It? (how-to paragraphs) 54
Why? Oh, Why? (cause-and-effect paragraphs) 55
Snakes or Dogs (compare-and-contrast paragraphs) 56
PLEASE!! (persuasive paragraphs) 57
Happy Birthday! (types of expository paragraphs) 58–59
Sweet Seasons (multiple paragraphs) 60
The Truth About Homework (five-paragraph essays) 61
Whale Tails and Whale Tales (recognizing stories) 62
Murray's Mix-Up (beginning, middle, end) 63
Where in the World? (settings) 64
Who's Who? (characters) 65
Who Said That? (characters) 66
What's the Problem? (problems) 67
Try, Try Again (events) 68
Final Reports (solutions) 69
One Small Light (story structure) 70–71
Look at It This Way (point of view) 72
A Million Questions (leads/hooks) 73
Mrs. Reid's Vase (story transitions) 74
The County Fair (descriptions) 75
What the Reader Sees (show, don't tell) 76
Show and Tell (action) 77
What's That, You Say? (dialogue) 78
Snow Day! (quotation marks) 79
The Grand Wedding (indenting quotes) 80
Fantastic Finishes (endings) 81
It's All in the Name (story titles) 82
Tell Me a Story (story elements) 83
Crash! Bang! Boom! (onomatopoeia) 84
Silly Safari Animals (alliteration and assonance) 85
Just Like That (similes) 86
The Angry River (personification) 87
What Shall I Write? (choosing a topic) 88
Prompt Me (prompts) 89
What a Plan! (planning expository writing) 90
My Dream Truck (description planning) 91
A Treasure Map (narrative planning) 92
The Moon (staying on topic) 93
Is That Your Mummy? (extraneous information) 94
A New Planet (elaboration) 95
That's Clear (specific writing) 96
Swamp Water (unclear references) 97
Vesuvius (revising fragments) 98
Too Many Little Ones (varying sentences) 99
Fishing with My Grandfather (editing verbs) 100
Apples for Everyone (editing spelling) 101
The Great Horse Escape (editing punctuation) 102
Awful Ads (editing capitalization) 103
Messy Monsters (editing paragraphing) 104
Favorite Fairy Tales (short answers) 105
The Odd Octopus (short answers) 106
What's the Point? (summaries) 107
The Lost City (summaries) 108
Mean Sam Clemm (book reports) 109
Take Note of This (taking notes) 110
Geysers of Yellowstone (taking notes) 111
Harriet Tubman (summarizing) 112
The Exxon *Valdez* (summarizing) 113
Dear Grandma (friendly letters) 114
An Invitation (friendly letters) 115
It's in the Mail (addressing envelopes) 116
A Couple of Couplets (poetry) 117
Two Crazy Cats (cinquains) 118
Loony Limericks (limericks) 119

Answer Key 120–128

identifying complete sentences   Name _____

Under the Sea

A **sentence** is a group of words that tells a complete thought.

sentences: The fish swam under the boat.
I saw him splash.
The water is cold.

not sentences: swimming by the rocks
a school of fish
in the middle of the ocean

Read each group of words. For each complete sentence, color the fish purple. If the group of words is not a sentence, color the fish green.

1. Fish eat worms.

2. at the bottom of the ocean

3. The whale lives in the deep water.

4. swims along the rocky shore

5. The ocean is very salty.

6. the great, white shark

7. Some seaweed floats.

identifying types of sentences   Name _____

Itty Bitty Bugs

A sentence that tells something is called a **statement**.
   Ladybugs don't wear dresses.
A sentence that asks something is called a **question**.
   Why do flies fly?
A sentence that shows strong emotion is called an **exclamation**.
   The bee stung me!
A sentence that gives an order is called a **command**.
   Hand me the butterfly net.
All sentences are complete thoughts.

Read each sentence. Write **statement**, **question**, **exclamation**, or **command** on each line to name the types of sentences.

1. _____ Why do you want to study bugs?

2. _____ Ants live in big groups called colonies.

3. _____ A butterfly starts its life as a caterpillar.

4. _____ Don't step on that beetle.

5. _____ That moth is big!

6. _____ How do crickets chirp?

7. _____ Some bugs bite.

8. _____ I caught a grasshopper!

9. _____ Take those bugs out of the house.

10. _____ Bugs live in many places on earth.

Published by Instructional Fair. Copyright protected.   IF87134 Building Writing Skills

capitals and end marks   Name _____

The Hike

Every sentence begins with a capital letter and ends with an end mark.
A **statement** ends with a period (.).
    We hike in the woods.
A **question** ends with a question mark (?).
    Did you hear a bird?
An **exclamation** ends with an exclamation point (!).
    There is a bear!
A **command** can end with a period or an exclamation point.
    Go back to the tent.   Run!

Rewrite each sentence. Add a capital letter at the beginning of each sentence. Add the correct end mark at the end of each sentence.

1. this trail is rocky and steep
   _____

2. i almost fell
   _____

3. juan wants to see some deer
   _____

4. did we bring water to drink
   _____

5. pick up that trash
   _____

6. who saw that hawk fly over the field
   _____

You're the author! On another sheet of paper, write one sentence of each type from above. Start with a capital letter and end with the correct end mark.

identifying complete sentences

A Trip to the Zoo

A **sentence** is a complete thought.
example: I want to go to the zoo today!
A **fragment** is not a complete thought. It is only part of a sentence.
example: very beautiful birds

Read each group of words. Circle the **S** if the words form a complete sentence. Circle the **F** if the words form a fragment.

S F 1. The zoo is a fun place to go!
S F 2. I love to see the snakes in the cages.
S F 3. into the alligator's pond
S F 4. Will you carry the popcorn?
S F 5. the tall zookeeper
S F 6. The lions are sleeping in the sun.
S F 7. That seal splashed me!
S F 8. while the monkeys play
S F 9. the black and white zebras
S F 10. Look at the teeth on that tiger!

Rewrite one fragment from above to make a complete sentence. Use a capital letter to begin each sentence. Choose a period(.), question mark(?), or exclamation point(!) to end each sentence.

11. _____
_____
_____

word order   Name _____

It's a Puzzle!

The words in a sentence must be in **order** to make sense.
wrong order: together Maria the puzzle put.
the puzzle put together Maria.
correct order: Maria put the puzzle together.

Rewrite the words in order to form a sentence that makes sense.

1. have puzzle a I jigsaw.
   _____

2. hundred has a It pieces.
   _____

3. John and help Oscar me.
   _____

4. puzzle This fun is!
   _____

5. crossword works puzzle Ahmed a.
   _____

6. He to stops help us.
   _____

7. a wooden puzzle builds Iko.
   _____

8. great all time have a We.
   _____

Published by Instructional Fair. Copyright protected.   IF87134 *Building Writing Skills*

subjects and predicates   Name _____

Peanut Butter and Jelly

All sentences have a **subject** and a **predicate**. The subject tells who or what the sentence is about.

examples: **My little sister** likes grape jelly.
                That bread tastes great.

The predicate tells what the subject does, has, or is.

examples: My little sister **likes grape jelly.**
                That bread **tastes great.**
                Jelly **is sweet.**

Draw a line to match each subject with the predicate that makes a complete sentence and makes the most sense. The first one is done for you.

1. My mom   sticks to the roof of my mouth.

2. Grape jelly   makes lunch for me.

3. Peanut butter   is good to drink with my sandwich.

4. Milk   is made from grapes and sugar.

5. I   is my favorite meal!

6. Chips and cookies   am eating lunch.

7. All my friends   like my sandwiches the best.

8. Lunch   are on my plate, too.

Published by Instructional Fair. Copyright protected.   IF87134 Building Writing Skills

subjects   Name _____

The Toy Store

All sentences have a subject and a predicate. The **subject** tells who or what the sentence is about.

examples: **My brother** likes toys.

His favorite toy is a red fire truck.

Circle the **subject** in each sentence.

1. The toy boat floats on the water.
2. I like to build with blocks.
3. The doll with the black hair is my favorite.
4. Tiny cars can zoom fast.
5. She wants a baseball mitt for her birthday.
6. The stuffed elephant is so nice!
7. Marbles come in different colors, shapes, and sizes.
8. That board game is too easy.

The **predicate** tells what the subject does, has, or is. Write your own **subject** to go with each predicate. Remember to begin each sentence with a capital letter.

1. _____ buys a present at the toy store.
2. _____ is only an inch tall.
3. _____ is so pretty!
4. _____ goes fast when you push it.
5. _____ is fun to build.

Published by Instructional Fair. Copyright protected.   IF87134 *Building Writing Skills*

predicates

Toys, Toys, Toys

The **predicate** tells what the subject does, has, or is.
examples: Tennis balls **bounce high**.
My best friend **has a toy truck**.
The stuffed cat **is my favorite**.

Underline the **predicate** in each sentence.

1. The dollhouse has real lights!
2. The jeep can drive over rocks and mud.
3. My sister loves toy horses.
4. The red car is the fastest.
5. A teddy bear makes a great gift.
6. I have a model plane.
7. Action games are fun.
8. This spaceship beeps loudly.

Write your own predicate to go with each subject. Remember to use the correct end mark.

1. The princess doll _____
2. Mandy and Mark _____
3. Hand puppets _____
4. Rocket cars _____
5. My mom and dad _____

Published by Instructional Fair. Copyright protected.   IF87134 *Building Writing Skills*

subjects and predicates　　　　　　　　　　　　　　Name _____

Once Upon a Time

Every sentence has a **subject** and a **predicate**. The **subject** tells who or what the sentence is about. The **predicate** tells what the subject does, has, or is.

subject:	predicate:
Little Red Riding Hood	is a sweet girl.
A mean witch	lived in the woods.
Jack	ran from Giant's house.

Circle the subject and underline the predicate in each sentence.

1. Cinderella worked hard.
2. Lon Po Po is a scary wolf.
3. The Blue Fairy turned Pinocchio into a real boy!
4. The Three Little Pigs had wolf stew.
5. Sleeping Beauty slept for a hundred years.
6. Snow White and Sleepy were friends.
7. The Three Billy Goats Gruff fooled the troll.
8. Goldilocks slept in the little bear's bed.
9. Anansi is a tricky spider.
10. Jack climbed the beanstalk.
11. Beast fell in love with Beauty.
12. Fairy tales are good stories.

You're the author! Write a story about a castle and a brave knight.

subjects and predicates   Name _____

Wild Wolves

Every sentence has a **subject** and a **predicate**. The subject tells who or what the sentence is about. The predicate tells what the subject does, has, or is.

subject:	**predicate:**
Wolves	live in packs.
Many people	are afraid of wolves.

Circle the subject and underline the predicate in each sentence.

1. Wolves have thick fur to keep them warm.
2. Dogs are related to wolves.
3. A den is a hole in the ground where wolves live.
4. Wolves eat meat.
5. Wolves hunt together as a pack.
6. Wolf pups play outside when they are three to four weeks old.
7. The alpha wolf is the strongest wolf in the pack.
8. A snarling wolf is angry.
9. Wolves can see well in the dark.
10. Some wolves live in the United States.
11. Many stories have a big, bad wolf.
12. Wolves are not really bad animals.

nouns and pronouns   Name _____

The Fire

A subject tells who or what the sentence is about. Every subject has a root **noun** or a **pronoun**. A noun is a person, place, or thing, such as **teacher**, **house**, or **cat**. A pronoun takes the place of a noun. Pronouns are words like **I**, **you**, **he**, **she**, **it**, **we**, or **they**.

examples: The **truck** is shiny and red.
　　　　　　　　The fire **station** is on the corner.
　　　　　　　　We like to talk to the fire chief.

Circle the subject in each sentence and write the root noun or pronoun on each line. The first one is done for you.

1. (The brave firefighters) are always ready to go.　　firefighters
2. A loud bell rings.
3. They slide down a tall pole.
4. One person drives the truck.
5. The siren is very loud.
6. We see the truck go by our house.
7. A spotted dog runs after the truck.
8. It stops at an old, empty house.
9. Thick, black smoke comes out of the windows.
10. Some firefighters point a hose at the house.
11. They shoot the water at the flames.
12. The firefighters put out the fire.
13. They are hot and tired.
14. Everyone cheers!
15. The fire truck goes back to the station.

action verbs   Name _____

Lights, Camera, Action!

The **predicate** always has a **verb**. The verb is a single word that tells what the subject does, has, or is. A verb can be an action word.

examples: The boy **writes** a scary story.
   Miranda **acted** in the play at school.
   The happy actor **smiles** at the camera.

Draw a line to match each picture to the correct action verb.

1.   runs

2.   has

3.   dances

4.   jumps

   is

5.   swings

   am

   sleeps

You're the author! Write a story about a sack race. Use seven action words.

Published by Instructional Fair. Copyright protected.   IF87134 *Building Writing Skills*

nonaction verbs   Name _____

Quiet, Please!

The predicate always has a **verb**. The verb is a single word that tells what the subject does, has, or is. A **nonaction verb** tells what a subject has or is.

examples: The library **has** many books.
I **am** a good reader.
She **was** late.

Complete each sentence with one of the nonaction verbs listed.

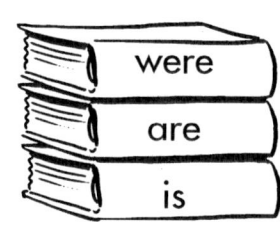

were   1. Mrs. Roose _____ the librarian.
are   2. We _____ at the library yesterday.
is   3. My friends _____ excited about reading.

4. This book _____ 152 pages.
5. Last week, Antone _____ to read three books.   has
6. I _____ *Charlotte's Web* by E.B. White.   have
                                                                    had

is   7. My mom _____ a writer.
am   8. Mrs. Roose _____ your book.
has   9. I _____ happy I found that book.

10. Every book _____ a secret.   is
11. You _____ the fastest reader I know.   are
12. The library _____ very big.   has

You're the author! Write about yourself, using six nonaction verbs.

Published by Instructional Fair. Copyright protected.   IF87134 *Building Writing Skills*

present-tense subject/verb agreement

How Does Your Garden Grow?

The verb in the sentence must agree with the subject. A **present-tense verb** tells what is happening right now. If the subject is one noun or pronoun (he, she, or it), add an **s** to the verb.

The **bird** eat**s** the seeds.   **He** plant**s** a flower.

She swing**s** high.   **It** look**s** like a worm.

If the subject is I, you, or more than one person, place, or thing, do not add an **s**.

I see a rainbow!   **Plants** grow in the sun.

You rake the leaves.   **We** work hard.

Read each sentence aloud. Circle the form of the verb that matches the subject.

1. I (like, likes) to water the vegetables.
2. This carrot (taste, tastes) the best.
3. The crows (eat, eats) the corn.
4. The scarecrow (scare, scares) them away.
5. A teeny, tiny spider (crawl, crawls) on the vine.
6. It (move, moves) fast!
7. The blue flowers (grow, grows) in the garden.
8. My friend (plant, plants) some seeds.
9. He (water, waters) the soil.
10. The plants (begin, begins) to grow.
11. We (enjoy, enjoys) our garden.
12. Do you (want, wants) a garden, too?

present tense—to be   Name _____

Going Up!

The verb **to be** is different from other verbs. These examples show how to make the subject and verb agree for the verb **to be** in the present tense.

    I am hungry   **He is** hungry.   **We are** hungry.
                        She is hungry.   **You are** hungry.
                        The dog is hungry. **They are** hungry.

Write the correct present-tense form of the verb **to be** to agree with the subject.

1. We _____ in the elevator.
2. I _____ talking to a tall man.
3. You _____ next to him.
4. The three little boys _____ very quiet.
5. They _____ going to the third floor.
6. The tall man _____ saying goodbye.
7. He _____ tired.
8. A girl _____ looking at the numbers.
9. She _____ going to the tenth floor.
10. She _____ happy.
11. Her dog _____ with her.
12. I _____ too hot.
13. The elevator _____ on the sixth floor.
14. We _____ getting off now.

past-tense regular verbs

Name _____

Ed, Ted, and Fred

A **past-tense verb** tells what has already happened. To put most verbs into the past tense, add **-ed** to the end of the verb. If the verb ends with an **e**, drop the **e** before adding the **-ed** ending.

examples: walk   walk**ed**
                explore   explor**ed**

Write the past tense of the verb on the line.

Ed likes to play baseball. He is friends with Ted and Fred. Yesterday,

they _____ to the park. They _____ to play baseball.
        walk   want

Ed _____ that his brother _____ his ball and bat.
    remember   use

He ran home with Ted to get them while Fred _____ at the park.
                                                             wait

Drops of rain _____ to fall. Fred met Ed and Ted at Ed's house
                  start

and they _____ milk and cookies as they _____ the
        enjoy   watch

rain from inside the house. Ed, Ted, and Fred _____ baseball the
                                                            play

next day after school.

past-tense irregular verbs   Name _____

Look Before You Leap

A **past-tense verb** tells what has already happened. Most verbs follow the **-ed** rule for past tense. Below are some **irregular verbs** that do not follow the **-ed** rule.

    came   made   gave   ran   went
    saw   ate   said   fell

Write the correct past-tense form of the irregular verb on the lily pad to help the frogs cross the river.

1. Yesterday, the frogs _____ to the edge of the river.
      come

2. They _____ some yummy bugs.
      eat

3. One green frog _____ the big bugs on the other side.
      see

4. He _____ that they could all cross the river.
      say

5. A yellow frog _____ and jumped.
      run

6. He _____ into the cold water.
      fall

7. The lily pads _____ the green frog an idea.
      give

8. He _____ a boat out of a lily pad.
      make

9. The little green frog _____ across the river.
      go

past tense—to be   Name _____

Monkey Business

The verb **to be** is different from other verbs. These examples show how to make the subject and verb agree using the verb **to be** in the past tense.

   I **was** glad.   He **was** glad.   We **were** glad.
                      She **was** glad.   You **were** glad.
                      The dog **was** glad.   They **were** glad.

Write the correct past-tense form of the verb **to be** to agree with the subject.

1. We _____ walking through the jungle.
2. I _____ very hungry.
3. You _____ very thirsty.
4. Six little monkeys _____ in a tree.
5. They _____ selling bananas and milk.
6. One monkey _____ holding a sign.
7. He _____ quiet.
8. Another monkey _____ peeling a banana.
9. She _____ excited.
10. You _____ going to buy some milk.
11. I _____ going to buy a banana.
12. We saw that the monkeys _____ packing little baskets.
13. One monkey _____ waving to us.
14. The rest of the monkeys _____ leaving.
15. "Come back!" we _____ shouting.
16. I think the monkeys _____ laughing!

Published by Instructional Fair. Copyright protected.   IF87134 Building Writing Skills

past-tense subject/verb agreement   Name _____

The Turtle's Trip

A **past-tense verb** tells what has already happened. Most verbs use the **-ed** ending to show past tense.

examples: walked   smiled   opened   helped

Irregular verbs do not follow the **-ed** rule.

examples: went   had   was   made   came

Choose the correct past-tense verbs to complete the story.

Tanya the Turtle _____ to go on a trip. She _____
                        want   know

that she _____ somewhere. She wanted to find a home. First, she
            belong

_____ to Scotland. The people _____ their food with
      go   share

Tanya. She _____ happy, but Scotland was too cold and rainy. Next
              be

she traveled to Africa. A boy _____ her find some water. She
                                    help

_____ the boy, but Africa was too hot. Finally, she _____
      love   come

to America. Tanya _____ across the states. She _____
                        walk   see

pretty places, but America was too big. Tanya _____ in her shell.
                                                    hide

Then, she _____. Tanya remembered that her shell was her home!
              smile

Published by Instructional Fair. Copyright protected.   IF87134 *Building Writing Skills*

compound subjects   Name _____

This and That

A **compound subject** is made up of two subjects joined by the word **and**.

cats + dogs = cats and dogs

Sentences with the same predicate may be joined into one sentence by using a **compound subject**.

example: Black cats play.
Spotted dogs play.
Black cats and spotted dogs play.

Combine the subjects to make a compound subject.

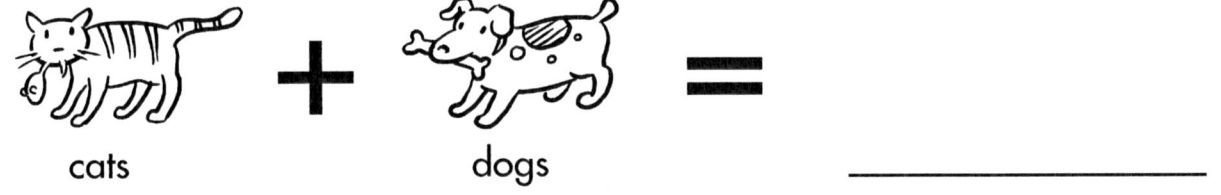

cats + dogs = _____

Combine the subjects of the two short sentences to write a new sentence with a compound subject.

1. Girls play baseball.
   Boys play baseball.

   _____

2. Penguins walk on snow.
   Seals walk on snow.

   _____

3. Red roses grow in the garden.
   Yellow tulips grow in the garden.

   _____

4. Ribbons make a gift look pretty.
   Bows make a gift look pretty.

   _____

compound predicates   Name _____

Read and Write

A **compound predicate** is made of two predicates joined by the word **and**.

　　　　　　read + write = read and write

Sentences with the same subject may be joined into one sentence by using a **compound predicate**.

example:　　　The boys read books.
　　　　　　　　The boys write stories.
　　　　　　　　The boys read books and write stories.

Combine these predicates to make a compound predicate.

sit　　+　　study　　=　　_____

Combine the predicates of the two short sentences to write a new sentence with a compound predicate.

1. Kayla runs.
   Kayla plays.

   _____

2. Wu adds numbers.
   Wu subtracts numbers.

   _____

3. Marena looks at a map.
   Marena finds her hometown.

   _____

4. Nakita goes to the library.
   Nakita checks out books.

   _____

compound sentences   Name _____

A Birthday Party

A simple sentence has a subject and a predicate. A **compound sentence** is made up of two simple sentences. They are joined by a comma and a connecting word such as **or**, **and**, or **but**. The connecting word is called a **conjunction**.

simple   Kevin scooped ice cream.

         Moni cut the cake.

compound   Kevin scooped ice cream**,** **and** Moni cut the cake.

Read each sentence. If the sentence is a compound sentence, circle the comma and the conjunction. For each compound sentence, color the correctly numbered birthday candle.

1. Marleen pops a balloon, and Eric jumps.
2. All the presents were in the hall.
3. Kiko blows a whistle.
4. Sabrina plays checkers, but Adam draws a picture.
5. The cake is chocolate, and the ice cream is vanilla.
6. Kris may sing alone, or everyone could sing together.
7. Mother tells everyone to come to the table.
8. Claire opens her presents, and Ali reads the cards.

You're the author! Write three compound sentences about a birthday party.

Published by Instructional Fair. Copyright protected.   IF87134 *Building Writing Skills*

compound sentences   Name _____

A Winter's Day

A simple sentence has a subject and a predicate. A **compound sentence** is made up of two simple sentences. They are joined by a comma and a connecting word like **or, and,** or **but**. The connecting word is called a **conjunction**.

simple: The air is cold.
              Snow is falling.

compound: The air is cold**, and** snow is falling.

Add a **comma** on the short line and the best conjunction (**or, and,** or **but**) on the longer line to finish each compound sentences.

1. We put on our heavy coats __ _____ we get out our mittens.
2. Shall we make a snowman __ _____ should we go sledding?
3. I am cold __ _____ I am still having fun!

Combine these simple sentences to make a compound sentence. Add a comma and the conjunction.

4. Juan makes a snow angel. (and)
   Anita makes snowballs.

   _____

5. Anita throws a snowball. (but)
   Juan just laughs.

   _____

Open any book and find a compound sentence. Write it on the lines below. Circle the comma and the conjunction.

6. _____
   _____
   _____

Published by Instructional Fair. Copyright protected.   IF87134 Building Writing Skills

run-on sentences   Name _____

The Best Day Ever

A **run-on sentence** is two or more sentences that run together without correct punctuation or conjunctions.

run-on: I woke up I was excited.
              I woke up, I was excited.

correct: I woke up. I was excited.
              I woke up, **and** I was excited.

Correct these run-on sentences by writing two shorter sentences.

1. I hopped out of bed the sun was shining.
   _____
   _____

2. My mom fixed pancakes I didn't have to go to school.
   _____
   _____

3. My dad wanted to go on a safari, I wanted to go, too.
   _____
   _____

4. We rode across the plains, I saw lions and elephants.
   _____
   _____

Correct these run-on sentences by adding a comma and a conjunction.

5. We stopped for dinner we ate zebra pie.
   _____

6. My mom tucked me into bed my dad read me a story.
   _____

Published by Instructional Fair. Copyright protected.   IF87134 Building Writing Skills

stringy sentences   Name _____

All Tied Up

A **stringy sentence** is one type of run-on sentence. It has too many ideas connected with **and, or, but,** or **so**. Make stringy sentences easier to read. Use no more than one **and, or, but,** or **so** in each sentence.

stringy: Mario wrapped the box and he tied the string around it and he wanted to mail it but he forgot the address.

correct: Mario wrapped the box. He tied the string around it. He wanted to mail it, but he forgot the address.

Draw a string around the packages with the stringy sentences.

1. I was tired, so I put my book away and I found my pajamas and I brushed my teeth and then I got into bed.

2. I was tired, so I put my book away. I found my pajamas and brushed my teeth. Then, I got into bed.

3. My brother drives a nice car. Sometimes he gives me a ride. One time he let me honk the horn. I hope he drives me home from school today.

4. My brother drives a nice car, and sometimes he gives me a ride, and one time he let me honk the horn and I hope he drives me home from school today.

5. Bears are very big so you have to be careful in the woods and never hike alone or bother a bear.

6. Bears are very big, so you have to be careful in the woods. Never hike alone or bother a bear.

stringy sentences   Name _____

Eli Is Excited!

Stringy sentences have too many ideas connected with **and, or, but,** or **so**. Make stringy sentences easier to read. Use no more than one **and, or, but,** or **so** in each sentence.

stringy: I want to learn to fly a plane, and one day I will drive a jeep, and I will be a safe driver, and I want to sail in a boat, too.

correct: I want to learn to fly a plane. One day I will drive a jeep and be a safe driver. I want to sail in a boat, too.

Eli gets so excited that he puts all his ideas into one sentence. Help him explain his ideas by breaking them into smaller sentences.

1. I will make the best game in the world and everyone will play and I will be the star and my friends will play, too.

   _____
   _____
   _____
   _____
   _____

2. I think the moon is made of cheese so we can send people to the moon and they can eat and then no one has to be hungry.

   _____
   _____
   _____
   _____
   _____

commas in a series   Name _____

Packing a Suitcase

Three or more words listed together are called a **series**. Use commas to separate words in a series. Use a conjunction (**and, or**) before the last word in a series.

examples: My family includes my **mom, dad, sister, and me**.

                  Fruit, sugar cookies, or crackers are our snack choices today.

Add commas to these sentences. The conjunctions have been added for you.

1. We are going on a trip to Japan China and Korea.
2. My mother father sister and I are packing our suitcases.
3. I need to pack my soap toothbrush and comb.
4. Mom, I can't find my socks shoes or underwear!
5. I can take my blue jeans green shorts and purple socks.
6. Do I need tennis shoes nice shoes or sandals?
7. A wallet a book and a watch are also good things to pack.
8. Should I pack a book a game or a yo-yo?
9. The tickets bags and maps are all ready.
10. Mom tucks me in kisses me and tells me good night.
11. Mom turns out the lights in my room the hall and the stairs.
12. I can't wait to travel play and have fun!

You're the author! Write a story about packing your own suitcase for a trip. Where are you going? What will you take? Use commas in your sentences to separate the things you will take with you.

adjectives

Name _____

Adjective Art

Adjectives are words that describe people, places, and things. They tell which one, what kind, and how many. To make your sentences clearer and more interesting, add describing words, or **adjectives,** to your writing.

The **green** paint is for the trees.

There are **three** apples on the ground.

Choose an adjective for each line to help the artist paint the picture below.

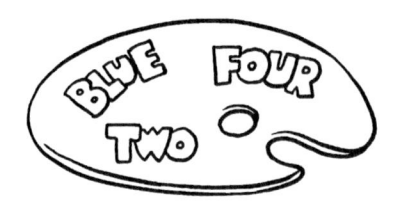

(Palette: BLUE, FOUR, TWO)

1. The painting has _____ trees.
2. The artist will paint a _____ dress.
3. The artist has _____ brushes.

4. The _____ trees are tall.
5. The _____ sun is in the sky.
6. The _____ clouds will be white.

(Palette: APPLE, PUFFY, YELLOW)

(Palette: THREE, RED, PRETTY)

7. _____ jars of paint are out.
8. The _____ paint is open.
9. The _____ painting is almost done.

adjectives adding   Name _____

Oh, Say, Can You See?

Adjectives are words that describe people, places, and things. They tell **which one, what kind,** and **how many.**

   The **holiday** parade passed by the **hardware** store.

When more than one adjective is used in a row, you sometimes need to use a comma to separate the adjectives. If you can say the word "and" between the two adjectives and it sounds fine, you need the comma.

   The **small** and **happy** children played in the park. (Needs a comma)

   The **small, happy** children played at the park.

   The **five** and **happy** children played in the park. (Doesn't need a comma)

   The **five happy** children played in the park.

Choose an adjective from the Word Bank to complete each patriotic sentence.

Word Bank
- blue
- courage
- Flag
- thirteen
- six
- red
- stars
- Star-Spangled
- fifty
- Old

1. The colors in the American flag are _____, white, and _____.
2. The flag has _____ stars and _____ stripes.
3. The seven red stripes stand for _____.
4. There are _____ white stripes.
5. The _____ stand for the fifty states.
6. _____ Day is on June 14th.
7. Another name for the American flag is _____ Glory.
8. "The _____ Banner" is the national anthem of the United States.

You're the author! Draw and color your own flag. Describe it using as many adjectives as you can. Answer these questions: What colors are in your flag? What shapes do you see? What do the shapes and colors mean?

how and when   Name _____

The Case of the Missing Grapes

Often a sentence can be made better by telling **how** or **when** the action was done.

How did Dexter wash the dishes?   He washed the dishes **slowly**.
When did you eat?   We ate **after lunch**.

Write a **how** or **when** question to fit each answer. Remember that a question is a complete sentence with a capital letter at the beginning and a question mark at the end. The first one is done for you. Then solve the mystery!

1. Caleb took a nap after lunch. _When did Caleb take a nap?_

2. Mr. Smith washed his hands at 2:30. _____

3. Kelly was very hungry. _____

4. Sven rushed to work in the morning. _____

5. Kelly read *Charlotte's Web* all afternoon. _____

6. Sam put the grapes away at 2:00. _____

7. Martha ate her lunch quickly. _____

8. Now answer this: Who took the grapes? (Hint: Grapes are sticky.) _____

You're the author! Write six questions and answers to solve another mysterious case.

where   Name _____

Hide and Seek

To explain or tell more in a sentence, include **where** words.
Often, more than one word is used to tell where.

examples: J.T. jumped **onto the boat**.

   My mom was cooking **outside**.

   The deer in the woods **ran away**.

Choose the correct word to complete each sentence and describe the picture.

Word Bank

in	on
behind	next
outside	above
under	along

1. The little boy playing _____ the box is Leroy.
2. Kevin is _____ the picnic table.
3. My sisters hide _____ the tree.
4. The bench _____ to the tree is white.
5. The woman _____ the bench is reading.
6. Birds fly _____ us.
7. We love to play _____ .
8. Patty rides a scooter _____ the path.

vivid verbs   Name _____

Save the Day

Some verbs are used too often, such as *went* or *said*. Changing an overused verb to an exciting or **vivid verb** can add more meaning to a sentence. It can also make your sentence more fun to read.

overused:	exciting:
went	skipped
went	zoomed
said	yelled
said	whispered

You are a superhero! Circle a vivid verb to complete each sentence. Write it on the line and save the day.

1. A train _____ into the tunnel. (went, zoomed)
2. A person was _____ to the tracks. (strapped, tied)
3. She _____, "Help!" (said, cried)
4. I _____ across the sky. (streaked, flew)
5. The train _____ louder. (seemed, roared)
6. Its headlight _____ brightly. (burned, was)
7. I _____ the girl just in time. (found, rescued)
8. I _____ her from the tracks. (got, pulled)
9. The train _____ past us. (went, thundered)
10. The girl _____, "You saved my life!" (shouted, said)

Published by Instructional Fair. Copyright protected.   35   IF87134 *Building Writing Skills*

cause and effect　　　　　　　　　　　　　　　　Name _____

Just Because

Adding an explanation to answer the question **why** helps the reader know more about what is happening in a sentence.

examples:　　　I took money to the store **to buy a pencil**.
　　　　　　　　　I like football **because it is fun**!

Explain why something happened by drawing a line between the two parts of the each sentence that match the best.

1. We didn't have school
2. I am going to the library
3. Everyone in class was happy
4. Jerry ran home from school

a. because our team won.
b. because it snowed so much.
c. to open his birthday mail.
d. to check out my favorite book.

5. All the dogs on my block barked
6. They didn't get good grades
7. The pie tasted bad
8. All our lights went out

e. because they saw a cat.
f. because of the big storm.
g. because it burned in the oven.
h. because they didn't study.

9. Carl took his medicine
10. I took my brother to the fair
11. Mom took a shower
12. Dad had to fix the car

i. to ride the merry-go-round.
j. because it had a flat tire.
k. so he would get better.
l. to clean up after her gardening.

You're the author! Write six sentences that tell why something happened.

the 5Ws + how   Name _____

Super Sentences!

You can make your sentences **super** sentences by telling **who, what, where, when, why,** and **how.**

　　regular sentence:　　The cat ran.
　　super sentence:　　The orange cat raced quickly up the fence to get away from the dog as she chased him.

Make some **super** sentences. Choose the right words from the choices below each sentence to tell where, when, why, and how. Fill in the blanks.

1. A tiny toad _____ hopped _____
   　　　　　　　　how　　　　　　　　　　　　where

   _____   _____ .
   　　　　　why　　　　　　　　　　　　　　when

   under the porch   quickly   when the rain started   to hide

2. The shiny rocket blasted _____ _____
   　　　　　　　　　　　　　　　how　　　　　where

   _____   _____ .
   　　　　　when　　　　　　　　　　　　　　why

   loudly   to go to Mars   this morning   into the air

3. The elves _____ fixed the cobbler's shoes _____
   　　　　　　　　how　　　　　　　　　　　　　　　　　　　where

   _____   _____ .
   　　　　　why　　　　　　　　　　　　　　when

   while he was sleeping   to help him   in his shop   quietly

You're the author! Write five super sentences that tell who, what, where, when, why, and how.

building sentences   Name _____

Under Construction

Building your sentences with the right words can give the reader more information and make your sentences more meaningful.

　　I ate a hamburger.

　　I **gobbled** a **giant** hamburger with **pickles, onions, and ketchup at the restaurant.**

Build good sentences by choosing the brick with the right words for each sentence. Rewrite the new sentence on the line. If the brick has a vivid verb, replace the old verb in the sentence.

1. The tall man walks. _____
_____
_____
_____
_____

Brick 1:
- softly
- in the den
- while sitting on Mom's lap

2. The kitten purred. _____
_____
_____
_____
_____

Brick 2:
- strolls slowly
- through the store
- looking for a new clock

3. A car went by our house. _____
_____
_____
_____
_____

Brick 3:
- raced by our house
- with three dogs chasing it
- late last night

complex sentences   Name _____

Ready, Set, Morph!

To make a sentence more interesting, you can sometimes change the order of the parts. Take the **when** or **where** part of the predicate and move it in front of the subject.

Columbus sailed the ocean blue **in 1492**.

In 1492, Columbus sailed the ocean blue.

Use a comma to separate the **when** or **where** part of the predicate from the subject. Reread the sentence to be certain it makes sense.

Rewrite these sentences. Move the **when** or **where** part of the predicate in front of the subject. Remember to add the comma.

1. Ice melts when it gets warm. _____

2. We have to behave at school. _____

3. We go to the cottage at the start of the summer. _____

4. The alien turned into a bug outside his spaceship. _____

5. Sometimes a rainbow comes out after it rains. _____

6. Kittens grow into cats with time. _____

paragraphs   Name _____

What's the Big Idea?

A **paragraph** is a group of sentences that tells the reader about one main idea.

   This is a paragraph:

   The topic sentence tells the main idea of a paragraph. Often, the topic sentence comes first. The rest of the sentences tell more about that idea. These are called supporting sentences. All of the sentences in a paragraph tell about one main idea.

Each group of words tells about a main idea. In each group, cross out the word that does not belong. Then, choose the main idea from the box below that best matches each group of words. Write it on the line.

1. boots   keys   running shoes   sandals
   main idea _____

2. beetles   ants   bees   snow
   main idea _____

3. paint   eggs   paper   brush
   main idea _____

Main Ideas
Bugs are everywhere.
Lunch is my favorite meal.
People wear many different things on their feet.
I love to paint.

You're the author! Write five words for this main idea: People have many kinds of pets.

extraneous details

Name_____

Field Day

A **paragraph** is a group of sentences that tells the reader about one main idea.

Many of these sentences are about the same main idea, or topic. Some of the sentences do not belong because they are not about Field Day. Cross out the sentences that do not belong.

Field Day is my favorite day at school.
Everyone comes to school ready to play.
I eat eggs and toast for breakfast.
First, my class gets to run a relay race.
We win because we are fast.
I like to play a computer racing game at home.
Sometimes we play tug-of-war with the teachers.
The teachers do not like to lose.
They pull hard, but we pull harder.
My teacher is very nice.
Finally, the students run around the school.
Our school was built in 1989.
This is the biggest race of the day.
We all run our fastest.
Mr. Lee is the history teacher.
It does not matter who wins.
We all have a good time on Field Day.

indentation   Name _____

Animal Addresses

   Paragraphs are separated by indentation. To **indent** means to move the first line of the paragraph in from the side. **The beginning of this paragraph is indented.** This tells the reader that a new **topic**, or idea, begins there.

Put an **X** on the blanks to show where the topic changes and a new idea begins. This is where a new paragraph should start.

   Some mice live in barns. They make tiny beds in the straw. _____ Lots of food can be found when the other animals are sleeping. A barn is a good place for a mouse house. _____ Other mice live in fields. A small hole in the ground makes a safe place to sleep. _____ Field mice eat grass, seeds, and flowers. Mice can be happy living in fields.

   The jungle is home to many animals. Birds and snakes live in the trees. Big cats and wild pigs roam on the ground. _____ Hundreds of fish swim in the jungle's rivers. The jungle gives these animals a safe place to live. _____ Jungles all over the world are in danger. People cut down the trees to get wood. _____ Others throw their trash in the rivers. People in nearby towns scare the animals away. Jungles are not as safe for animals as they used to be.

Check it out! Look in any book. You will find paragraphs separated by indentation or by a space between paragraphs. Both of these tell the reader when the main idea changes.

topic sentences   Name

Topics in the Tropics

The main idea of a paragraph is called the topic. One sentence usually tells what the topic is. It is called the **topic sentence**. Often, the topic sentence is the first one in the paragraph.

Underline the topic sentence in each paragraph.

Parrots are beautiful birds that live in the tropics. They like the hot jungles. A parrot's beak is strong for breaking nuts to eat. Sometimes the birds sit on the branches of trees and eat fruit. Parrots spread their colorful feathers to stay cool.

My family is having a luau. A luau is a kind of party from Hawaii. We are going to roast a pig. There will be lots of pineapple, too. After dinner, my dad will light a big fire. Everyone will do the hula dance. We are excited about it.

Have you ever been to Hawaii? Hawaii is an interesting place. It is a group of islands. Very old volcanoes made the islands. Hawaii has jungles and cities. It also has lots of beaches. Hawaii is in the Pacific Ocean.

topic sentences   Name _____

Up, Up, and Away

The main idea of a paragraph is called the topic. One sentence usually tells what the topic is. It is called the **topic sentence**. Often, the topic sentence is the first one in the paragraph.

Each paragraph below needs a topic sentence. Circle the letter of the best topic sentence.

1. a. A pilot can fly a balloon. b. Hot air balloon rides are fun.

    First, you climb into the basket. You might feel a little scared. Next, the pilot turns on the fire to heat the air in the balloon. There is a big blasting noise, and the basket begins to rise. When the ropes are cut, the balloon floats away. You can see a long distance, and everything looks beautiful. There is nothing like a hot air balloon ride!

2. a. Hot air balloons are beautiful. b. Hot air balloons are easy to fly.

    Some are just one color, such as red, blue, or yellow. Others have pretty designs. When there is a balloon race, a hundred balloons can fill the sky with their colors. Sometimes, a single green balloon floats in the blue sky. Whether there is one balloon or one hundred, all the balloons are lovely as they move across the sky.

3. Write your own topic sentence for this paragraph: _____

    _____

    First, you have to learn how to take care of the balloon. The next thing to learn is how to take off and land. Finally, you must know about the wind. The wind will steer your balloon. These are some of the things you need to know to fly a balloon.

supporting sentences   Name _____

Lean on a Friend

A topic sentence tells the main idea in a paragraph. **Supporting sentences** explain more about the main idea.

Read each sentence. Which sentence tells a main idea? Which sentences support the main idea? Write the word **topic** before each topic sentence. Write **supporting** before each supporting sentence.

1. _____ Friends can make a bad day good.
2. _____ Sometimes, all it takes is a nice smile.
3. _____ On other days, only a hug will work.

4. _____ My best friend is different from my other friends.
5. _____ His name is Bandit.
6. _____ Bandit is an old raccoon who lives by the river.

Write two supporting sentences for each topic sentence.

I miss my best friend. _____
_____
_____
_____

Friendship is the greatest thing in the world. _____
_____
_____
_____

Published by Instructional Fair. Copyright protected.   45   IF87134 Building Writing Skills

examples   Name _____

Perfect Pizza

The topic sentence in a paragraph tells the main idea. **Supporting sentences** explain more about the main idea. Some supporting sentences give examples.

Read the paragraph below. On each pizza slice is a supporting sentence with an example. Write each supporting sentence where it fits best in the paragraph.

- Pizza comes eight slices to a box.
- My favorites are pepperoni and black olives.
- The cheese is melted, and steam rises from the pizza.

Pizza is my favorite food for three reasons. First, it is hot and bubbly.

_____

_____

Second, the toppings are great!

_____

_____

Third, pizza is easy to share.

_____

_____

Pick up a slice, and you're ready to eat. I think pizza is perfect!

Write your own examples for these sentences:

Once, someone gave me the perfect gift. _____

_____

Today, the weather was perfect! _____

_____

transitions

Build a Bridge

Transition words help the reader follow the main idea. They can show the order of things. They also show how different ideas are connected.

order: first, second, third, then, finally
connection: one, another, often, therefore

Circle all the transition words in the paragraph.

The Golden Gate Bridge was built across a large bay. First, the workers had to make a platform from concrete blocks under the water. Second, the two towers were built. These took many years to make. Then, giant cables were hung between the towers. The cables are as thick as cars. Finally, the rest of the bridge had to hang from the cables. This is a special kind of bridge called a suspension bridge. People all over the world know about the Golden Gate Bridge.

Write the correct transition words on the lines to finish the following paragraph.

Today   Another   Often   One

People built bridges long ago just like they do today. _____ reason they built bridges was to travel to other towns. _____ reason may have been to get their crops. _____ , they built bridges over water or across cliffs. In the past, bridges have helped people to live. _____ , bridges still help people in their daily lives.

sequencing   Name _____

In the Kitchen

In some paragraphs, the order of the sentences is very important. Clues, such as transition words, tell the order of the sentences.

examples: first, next, after, then, finally

The sentences in these two paragraphs are all mixed up. Put them in order by writing numbers in each box.

- ☐ Then, stir and enjoy!
- ☐ Making lemonade is easy.
- ☐ First, mix three spoons of powder into a glass of water.

- ☐ Then, get the peanut butter, honey, and powdered milk.
- ☐ To make peanut-butter bars, you first need to wash your hands.
- ☐ Third, get a large bowl and a big, strong spoon.
- ☐ Measure one cup of peanut butter, one cup of honey, and two cups of powdered milk. Place them in the bowl.
- ☐ When it is mixed well, put it in a pan.
- ☐ Cut into squares, and eat!
- ☐ Then, stir the mixture carefully.

You're the author! Ask a family member if you may look at a cookbook. Find a recipe with a few steps. Look at the transition words used in the recipe.

concluding sentences   Name _____

Great Endings

A **concluding sentence** comes at the end of the paragraph. It tells the main idea in a different way, or it gives the reader something to think about.

Underline the concluding sentence in each paragraph.

1. You should read *Charlotte's Web* by E.B. White. It is about a pig named Wilbur and his spider friend, Charlotte. The two friends share many adventures. The end is both sad and happy. You will love this book.

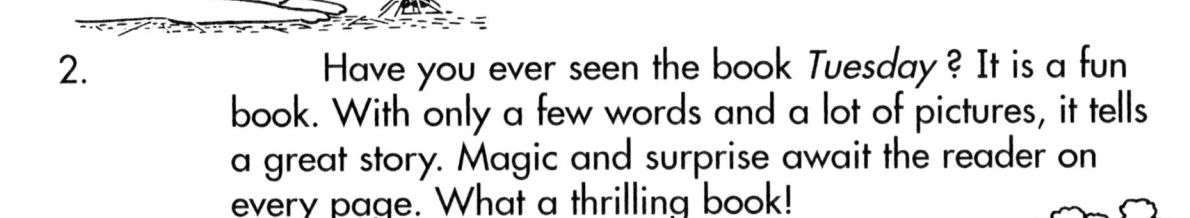

2. Have you ever seen the book *Tuesday*? It is a fun book. With only a few words and a lot of pictures, it tells a great story. Magic and surprise await the reader on every page. What a thrilling book!

3. I think everyone should read *The Magic Tree House* books. Jack and Annie are great characters. I also like their tree house. When the tree house spins, I know a wild adventure will begin. The best part of each book takes place after the adventure, when they come back home. Wouldn't you like to go on an adventure with Jack and Annie?

You're the author! Write a paragraph about your favorite book. Remember to write a topic sentence, supporting sentences, and a concluding sentence.

concluding sentences   Name _____

End of the Day

A **concluding sentence** comes at the end of the paragraph. It tells the main idea in a different way, or it gives the reader something to think about.

Each paragraph below needs a concluding sentence. Circle the letter of the best concluding sentence. Notice that each paragraph is indented.

1.   I think evening is the most beautiful time of day. As the sun sets, the sky turns shades of red or purple. The first stars peek out of the night. Sometimes, the moon rises before the sun is gone. Lights begin to come on all across the town. A yellow glow shines through windows and doors. The whole town looks beautiful.

    a. Sometimes, it's too cloudy. b. Evening is a great end to the day.

2.   Mr. Lopez works hard all day. He builds airplanes. He works on the landing gear all morning. By lunch, Mr. Lopez is ready for a rest. He works on the tail during the afternoon. His work is hard.

    a. Airplanes are heavy.   b. At the end of the day, Mr. Lopez is tired.

3. Write your own concluding sentence for this paragraph.

         I cannot wait for bedtime tonight. Normally, I don't like to go to bed, but my dad started reading *Peter Pan* to me. I think about the story all day long. We will read about Captain Hook's ship tonight.

    _____
    _____
    _____
    _____

expository paragraphs   Name _____

Horsing Around

An **expository paragraph** gives information or explains something.

1. This paragraph states what the writer likes about horses. Use the sentences in the list to complete the paragraph. Write the sentences in order on the lines.

    Second, I love to ride horses.
    Third, horses are very smart.
    First, they are beautiful animals.

    Even though I like all animals, horses are my favorite.

    _____
    _____
    _____

    Horses are the best animals I know.

2. One way to make a paragraph better is to give examples for each idea. Add the examples from the list where they belong to complete the paragraph.

    They understand all kinds of commands.
    I like to gallop in the woods.
    They have bright eyes and shiny coats.

    Even though I like all animals, horses are my favorite.
    First, they are beautiful animals. _____
    _____
    Second, I love to ride horses. _____
    _____
    Third, horses are very smart. _____
    _____
    Horses are the best animals I know.

Published by Instructional Fair. Copyright protected. 51 IF87134 *Building Writing Skills*

informative paragraphs   Name _____

Sssssssssnakes!

An expository paragraph gives information or explains something. One type of expository writing is an **informative paragraph**. It gives information.

Only five of these sentences belong in this paragraph. Cross out the sentences that do not belong. Rewrite the paragraph. Remember that a paragraph has a topic sentence.

There are many kinds of snakes. Kenny has two snakes. Some pythons are as long as a bus. Water snakes live in rivers or lakes. The snake at the zoo is named Monty. Garter snakes are very small. I like snakes. All snakes are reptiles.

_____
_____
_____
_____
_____
_____
_____
_____
_____
_____
_____

You're the author! Write an informative paragraph about your family. Begin with this topic sentence: I have a special family.

descriptive paragraphs   Name _____

Stripes or Spots?

Expository writing gives information or explains something. A **descriptive paragraph** paints a picture in the reader's mind. It describes something.

Below is an idea web. The main idea is in the center and the examples or details are around the outside.

- type:
- size:
- color:
- pattern:

(center: the snake I want)

Fill in the details by writing the words below where they belong in the web.

stripes   garter snake   black   small

Now use the ideas in the web to complete the paragraph. Remember that the main idea is in the topic sentence.

   I want a snake for a pet. A _____ would make a great
pet. They are _____ so I would not need a big cage.
                     size   type
Many garter snakes are _____. I would like a black one with
                              color
_____ all the way down its back. That would be a great pet.
     pattern

You're the author! Write a descriptive paragraph about your favorite dinner. Use words that tell how it looks, smells, sounds, feels, and tastes.

Published by Instructional Fair. Copyright protected.   53   IF87134 Building Writing Skills

how-to paragraphs   Name _____

How Do You Do It?

Expository writing gives information or explains something. A **how-to paragraph** explains the steps of how to do something.

This paragraph explains how to take care of a snake. Put the sentences in the right order and write them on the lines to complete the paragraph. Two sentences in the list follow each other.

   Also, when you touch a snake, always pet it from head to tail.

   Then, set up your cage with a small bowl of water and a heat lamp.

   Finally, different kinds of snakes eat different kinds of food.

   First, you need a glass cage, a heat lamp, food, and some water.

   Before bringing your snake home from the pet store, you should know a few things. _____

_____

_____

_____

You may want to put rocks, sticks, and grass in the cage, too. _____

_____

Petting a snake the wrong way will hurt its scales. _____

_____

Make sure you ask about the kind of food your snake needs. A snake is a great pet if you know how to take care of it.

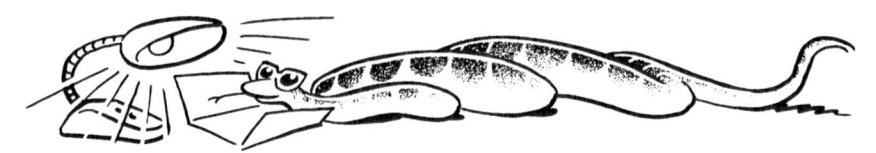

You're the author! Write a paragraph about how to brush your teeth. Remember, your steps must be in order.

cause-and-effect paragraphs   Name _____

Why? Oh, Why?

Expository writing gives information or explains something.

A **cause-and-effect paragraph** explains why something happened.

Draw a line to match each cause to its effect. Notice that the cause happens before the effect.

Cause

1. Don't pet a snake in the wrong direction, from tail to head.
2. Snakes should not be kept in a cold place.
3. Never feed a snake something it should not eat.

Effect

a. The wrong food will make a snake sick.
b. Doing this could hurt its scales.
c. A snake cannot make itself warm, and it could get sick.

Read the cause-and-effect paragraph below. Underline the causes. Circle the effects. (Hint: There are three of each.)

   I have to watch my snake, Jake, more closely. Yesterday, I took him out of his cage to clean it. He got away when I was not looking. He slithered as fast as lightning into the kitchen. My mom screamed loudly and jumped on a chair. Jake hid under the stove. I looked for a long time before I found him. Now he is back in his cage. Next time, I plan to put him in a box while I clean his cage!

compare-and-contrast paragraphs   Name _____

Snakes or Dogs

Expository writing gives information or explains something. A paragraph that tells how things are the same or different is called a **compare-and-contrast paragraph**.

This is a Venn diagram. It is used to show how things are the same or different. Write the ideas in the Venn diagram where they belong. Three are done for you.

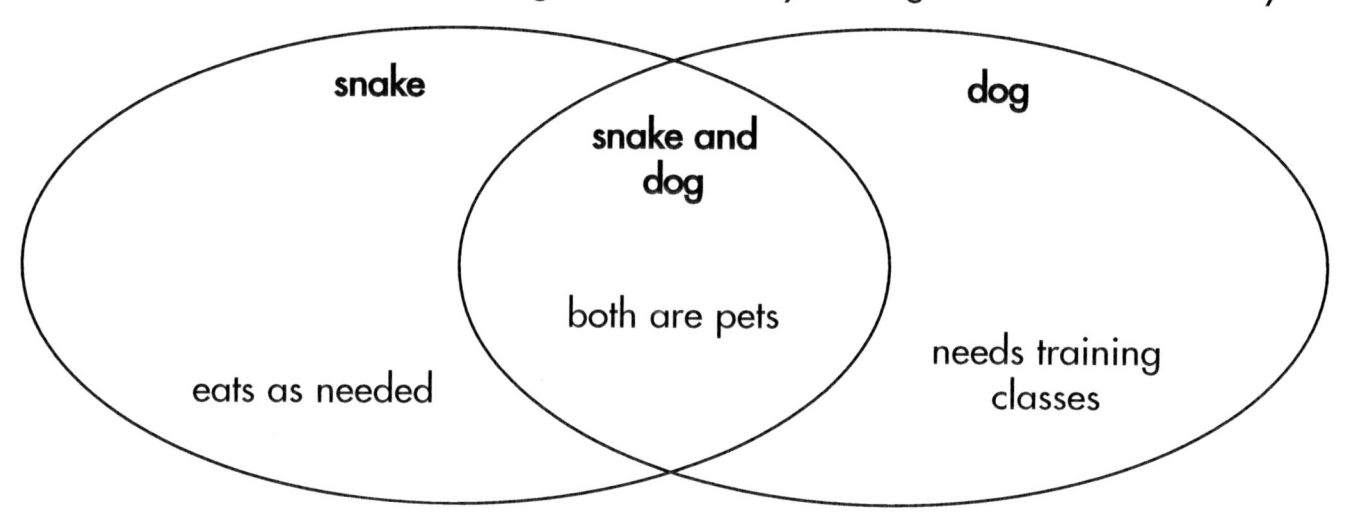

snake — eats as needed

snake and dog — both are pets

dog — needs training classes

~~both are pets~~   needs to go for walks   eats every day
needs a heat lamp   both need care   no training classes
~~needs training classes~~   both are fun   ~~eats as needed~~

Use the information in the Venn diagram to complete this compare-and-contrast paragraph.

    Even though snakes and dogs are both good pets, they are different in many ways. A dog _____ every day, but a snake only eats as needed. Both pets have special needs. A dog needs to go for _____. A snake needs a _____ lamp. Another difference is that dogs need training classes and snakes don't. Both of these pets are fun to have.

Published by Instructional Fair. Copyright protected.   56   IF87134 *Building Writing Skills*

persuasive paragraphs   Name _____

PLEASE!!

Expository writing gives information or explains something. In a **persuasive paragraph**, the writer tries to talk the reader into something.

Here is a list of thoughts about having a snake as a pet. Some of the thoughts are reasons for having a snake. Some are reasons against having a snake. Write the words **for** or **against** in front of each sentence to show what kind it is.

1. _____ It is easy to take care of snakes.
2. _____ Snakes do not shed fur all over the house.
3. _____ Mom does not want to feed a snake.
4. _____ My sister is afraid of snakes.
5. _____ Snakes do not need to go for walks.
6. _____ You do not have to train a snake to be good.
7. _____ Snakes need a heat lamp at all times.
8. _____ Snakes are quiet.

Use the reasons for having a snake to write a persuasive paragraph. Remember, you are trying to talk someone into something.

    Although Mom and Dad do not want a snake, I think a snake is a great pet. This is why I would like to have a snake. _____

_____

_____

_____

_____

identifying types of expository paragraphs   Name _____

Happy Birthday!

These are all expository paragraphs.

Read each paragraph. Find the box that describes that type of paragraph. Write the type of paragraph on each line.

1. _____

   Mom and Dad, I think I should be able to have a birthday party for three reasons. First, I think it would be fun to spend time with my friends. We also have not had cake and ice cream lately. My sister and brothers would enjoy the party, too. Surely, it is a good idea to have a party.

2. _____

   This is how I can invite all my friends to my birthday party. My dad and I will buy invitations at the store. The first thing I will do is to write the day and time inside each invitation. Next, I will write each friend's name on the outside of each envelope. Last, I will give them to my friends. I cannot wait for the party!

3. _____

   I wonder if I should ask for a puppy or a video game. Both would be fun to have, but a dog would take a lot of care. A video game cannot snuggle at night, but it takes very little care. A dog has many other costs, such as food, vets, and grooming. I think the video game would be best for me.

Compare-and-Contrast Paragraph
- topic sentence
- first comparison or contrast
- second comparison or contrast
- third comparison or contrast
- concluding sentence

Persuasive Paragraph
- state opinion
- first reason for
- second reason for
- third reason for
- concluding sentence

How-To Paragraph
- topic sentence
- materials
- first step
- second step
- third step
- concluding sentence

identifying types of expository paragraphs   Name _____

Happy Birthday! (cont.)

These are all expository paragraphs.

Read each paragraph. Find the box that describes that type of paragraph. Write the type of paragraph on each line.

4. _____

What a beautiful birthday cake I have! Mom made it look just like a puppy. It has floppy ears with a shiny, black gumdrop nose. The dog cake even has a blue frosting collar that says "Snoopy." When I saw the cake, I was sure I am getting a video game. I think Mom and Dad are hinting that my cake is the only dog I'm going to get.

5. _____

My birthday cake was nearly ruined. First, Felix tried to pin the tail on the cat. The poor cat ran through the kitchen and jumped up on the table. Mom grabbed the cake just before the cat ran into it. We almost had a cat in our dog cake!

6. _____

I had my birthday party on Saturday. Four boys and three girls came to the party. Everyone had a piece of my dog birthday cake with a scoop of vanilla ice cream. My parents gave me a white beagle puppy named "Snoopy." Everyone who came to the party said that it was really fun, and they all loved my new dog!

Informative Paragraph
- topic sentence
- first fact
- second fact
- third fact
- concluding sentence

Descriptive Paragraph
- topic sentence
- descriptive sentence
- descriptive sentence
- descriptive sentence
- concluding sentence

Cause-and-Effect Paragraph
- topic sentence
- cause or effect
- cause or effect
- cause or effect
- concluding sentence

multiple paragraphs   Name _____

Sweet Seasons

A **paragraph** is a group of sentences that tells the reader about one main idea. It has a topic sentence, supporting sentences, and a concluding sentence.

When writing **more than one paragraph**, the first sentence of the first paragraph tells the reader the topic. Supporting sentences tell more about the topic. There is no concluding sentence because the writer has more ideas.

The next paragraph begins with a topic sentence that has a transition. This helps the reader to know that there is a new idea. Supporting sentences tell more about the new idea.

Only the last paragraph needs to have a concluding sentence.

Read these paragraphs. Underline the topic sentence in each paragraph. Remember that the topic sentence in each second paragraph has a transition. Circle the concluding sentence.

My two favorite seasons are winter and spring. Winter is white with snow. The cold air feels good on my cheeks. I enjoy making snowmen. I love drinking hot chocolate in front of the fire.

Winter is fun, but spring is beautiful! Spring is when the flowers bloom. The sun shines brighter, and birds fill the trees. The world wakes up from a long nap. Winter and spring are truly the best seasons.

Even though summer means no school, it's my least favorite season. I really like school. I get to see my friends every day. In the summer, my best friend goes to her aunt's house. We don't see each other for months.

It's great to relax, but summer is usually too hot and humid. On some days, there's a cool breeze, but those days seem few and far between.

I'll take winter and spring over summer any day!

five-paragraph essays   Name _____

The Truth About Homework

A **five-paragraph essay** is almost like a stretched-out paragraph. The topic sentence stretches to the first paragraph, the **introduction**. The supporting sentences become the paragraphs in the **body** of the essay. The concluding sentence becomes the last paragraph, or **conclusion**.

Paragraph	**Essay**
topic sentence	introduction
supporting sentences	body paragraphs
concluding sentence	conclusion

Read the simple paragraph and the essay. Match each sentence in the single paragraph to a paragraph in the essay.

Paragraph

a. Children should not have too much homework. **b.** By the time they get home, they need some time to rest. **c.** They need to run and play for a while. **d.** Family time is very important, too. **e.** If children spend all their time on homework, they will miss other important times.

Essay

____ 1. Children should not have too much homework. They need rest. They also need play time and family time. These things make them happy and healthy.

____ 2. First, time to rest is important for healthy children. Children need a break after school. This break gives their minds a rest, and it helps get them ready for the next day.

____ 3. Children need time to run and play, too. Playing with friends is a way to learn important lessons. They learn how to share, listen, and get along. They also get good exercise in this way.

____ 4. Finally, families are great teachers of children. Talking together is how children learn to love and care about others. Children need this happy time at home.

____ 5. Children need rest time. They need play time. They also need family time. Too much homework can take these important times away.

recognizing stories   Name _____

Whale Tails and Whale Tales

A **narrative** tells a story. A story can be about real life, or it can be made up. **Expository** writing gives information or explains something.

Write the word **narrative** above each paragraph that tells a story. Write the word **expository** above each paragraphs that gives information or explains something.

1. _____

   A mean, old shark named Gobbles made fun of Elvis. Elvis was a purple whale. Gobbles laughed because Elvis was not the same as the other whales. While Gobbles was laughing, Yoko the sea turtle swam past him. She told Gobbles to be nice. Then, she winked and said that Elvis was cute. Elvis smiled as Gobbles swam away.

2. _____

   Killer whales sometimes act like wolves or lions. Often, these whales live in groups like packs of wolves. They also hunt together the way lions hunt. In a pack, these whales can hunt a giant blue whale. Killer whales live in the sea, but they behave like some animals found on land.

3. _____

   Tuesday, I saw a whale in the sky. She was a puffy, white whale and she followed me home from school. The whale swam across the blue sky and even blocked the sun. When I got home, I watched my whale swim over the city. She turned dark and blew a big wind through the trees. Then, my whale cloud rained on the city.

beginning, middle, end

Name _____

Murray's Mix-Up

A **narrative** is a story. Like expository writing, a story has a **beginning** (introduction), a **middle** (body), and an **end** (conclusion).

narrative:	expository:
beginning	introduction
middle	body
end	conclusion

Murray dropped his notebook. Pages from his stories fell onto the floor. Help Murray by writing **beginning**, **middle**, or **end** before each story section.

1. _____ Once upon a time in a land far away, there lived a very rich king and his stubborn son.

2. _____ It was just as my grandfather always said, "All's well that ends well!"

3. _____ Even the second time, I thought it was just a shadow. But then, out of the corner of my eye, I saw it!

4. _____ They all lived happily ever after.

5. _____ The racecar roared down the track. This was it. This was the race that Jefferson had waited for his whole life.

6. _____ It all started the summer I turned ten.

7. _____ When we woke up, the storm was over. The neighborhood was a mess, but we were all safe. A soft "meow" came from the hall closet. So Stripes hadn't been out in the storm after all! She had found her own safe place.

settings

Where in the World?

The **setting** is where and when a story takes place.

Read the beginnings of these stories. Circle the letters in front of the words that tell when and where the story takes place.

Lumpy oinked and sniffed around for some corn. This was his third morning at the fair, and he was hungry. He could smell popcorn, pie, and cotton candy from his pen, and that made him even hungrier.

1. Where does this story take place?

    a. at the fair

    b. on a farm

2. When does this story take place?

    a. on Saturday

    b. in the morning

Three years ago, I went to Zbot, a small planet far from Earth. On Zbot, I met a short, green alien named Gronk. Gronk was the happiest alien in the universe. He always had three smiles on his face.

3. When does this story take place?

    a. in the future

    b. three years ago

4. Where does this story take place?

    a. in a spaceship

    b. on planet Zbot

Write **where** and **when** this story beginning takes place.

Tiny Toaster looked across the room. The kitchen was always scary in the dark. Even the little light over the stove didn't help tonight. Tiny wrapped his cord around himself. He always felt safer that way.

5. where: _____

6. when: _____

characters   Name _____

Who's Who?

Characters are the people, animals, or things in a story. Writers can describe what the characters look like. They can also tell how the characters think, act, and talk.

Match each paragraph about a character to the right picture.

____ 1. Hector is nine years old. He has curly black hair. When he smiles, his cheeks round out and his eyes sparkle.

a.

____ 2. On weekends, Carlo works on his dad's fishing boat. Carlo always wears a rubber hat, just like his father. He loves their time together.

b.

____ 3. Dee is always plotting something. Her mind just goes, goes, goes. If you look into her eyes, you can see her scheming. That girl is up to no good.

c.

____ 4. Judge James sat behind his desk. He was tired. The day had been long and hard. He took off his glasses and rubbed his eyes.

d.

____ 5. Trina loves sports! Surfing and bike riding are her favorites. She always has a big smile on her face and her favorite baseball cap on her head.

e.

You're the author! Write a short paragraph about a character. Describe what the character looks like. Also, tell how the character thinks, acts, and speaks. Draw a picture of your character to go with your paragraph.

characters

Who Said That?

Characters can be people, animals, or things. A story tells what the characters do. We get to know the characters by how they think, act, and talk.

Characters are often described by the way they talk or think. Write the words or thoughts for each character. Use the Idea Bank to fill in the blanks.

1. Mr. O'Hara is our next-door neighbor. He is 87 years old. He always tells us that _____

2. Yesterday, the principal told the students that _____

3. Li walked with his lunch tray through the cafeteria. When someone bumped him, his tray and all his food spilled to the floor. He thought to himself that _____

4. Angelina was worried about her math test. She feared _____

5. From inside the space shuttle, Lorna could see the whole world. Later, she told her friends that _____

Idea Bank

this was not his lucky day.

he remembers the day each one of us was born.

there was never a more beautiful sight.

she wouldn't do well, even though she had studied.

they could get hurt if they run in the halls.

problems   Name _____

What's the Problem?

In every story, the **main character** has a problem. The story shows how the main character finds a solution to the problem.

Read the beginnings to these stories. Circle the letter that best describes the main character's problem.

1. Kyu's stomach growls. He has only eaten a few handfuls of berries in the past two days. The island he is on does not have much food to eat. Kyu sees some small, furry animals. He wonders what he would do if he could catch one.

   a. Kyu is sad.
   b. Kyu's boat sank.
   c. Kyu needs to find food.

2. Swoop rode the warm air high into the sky. A few slow beats with his wings pushed him farther ahead of the coming storm. He had never come so far over the hills, and he couldn't remember how to get back home. A crash of thunder pounded the air behind him. Swoop flew faster. Now he was really scared.

   a. Swoop hates rain.
   b. Swoop is lost, and a storm is coming.
   c. The hills are too big.

3. A green van pulled up in front of 8020 Chester Road. The old house stood a little straighter. Her windows gleamed as the young family came up her walk. Would this be the family to stay? She held her breath when they opened the door and stepped into the hallway.

   a. The house is lonely.
   b. The family is too young.
   c. The house needs new paint.

You're the author! Write the beginning of a story. Remember to include a setting, characters, and a problem.

events   Name _____

Try, Try Again

The **events** in a story are the ways the character or characters try to solve the problem. These attempts do not solve the problem.

Read each problem statement. Then, circle the letter of the paragraph that tells about an **event**, an attempt to solve the problem.

1. Problem: The secret agent, 003, left his spy camera on the train.

   a. Agent 003 watched as the train pulled from the station. He bolted out to the parking lot and hopped onto his motorcycle. Within a few minutes, he was racing alongside the train. He reached out to grab a handrail on the train. Just then, he saw the bridge. He skidded to a stop. He would have to find another way.

   b. Agent 003 watched as the train pulled from the station. He had to get those pictures. They showed that King Kalam was alive. Without the pictures, nobody would know. Agent 003 scowled as he thought. How could he get the camera back?

2. Problem: Isabel ripped her dance costume for the school play.

   a. The costume was beautiful. The top was made of shiny, pink cloth. It had long sleeves and sparkles. The skirt was long and had more sparkles. A thin, gold crown finished the look. Under the lights on the stage, Isabel's costume glowed.

   b. Isabel was sad when she saw the rip. She knew she had to fix it before the play. After she changed into her jeans and top, Isabel put the costume on the table. She ran to her craft box. Inside, Isabel found some tape. She tried to tape the dress, but the tape didn't stick. She frowned.

You're the author! Write another attempt to solve either problem above.

solutions   Name _____

Final Reports

The **solution** in the story is the way the problem is solved. Sometimes the main character solves the problem. Sometimes the problem is solved in other ways.

Read the problem statement. Then, decide if each following passage is an event or a solution. Remember, an **event** is an attempt to solve a problem. A **solution** solves the problem. Write **event** or **solution** on the line before each passage.

1. Problem: I forgot my report that was due today.

    a. _____ I asked my teacher if I could go home to get it at lunchtime. She said I could not leave school until the end of the day, even to get my report.

    b. _____ I called my mom, but she was not home. She could not bring it to me. I didn't know what else I could do!

    c. _____ In science class, someone from the office brought me my report. Mom brought it into school. She must have seen it sitting on the table. Thank you, Mom!

These events and solution are mixed up. Number them in the correct order.

2. Problem: The radio reported that five monkeys escaped from the zoo.

    a. _____ A wildlife expert and her staff came to help. At last, the monkeys were caught and returned to their home at the zoo.

    b. _____ Someone saw the monkeys at the grocery store. By the time the animal catchers arrived, the monkeys had run over the roof and were gone.

    c. _____ Later, in a small movie theater, the five monkeys appeared. Some people tried to catch them, but the monkeys were too fast. They toppled popcorn and sodas on their way out the doors, making wild monkey noises as they ran.

story structure

One Small Light

The way a story is put together is called the **story structure**. The setting, characters, and problem are usually explained in the beginning of the story. The events are in the middle of the story. The problem is solved at the end of the story.

Read the story. Then, complete the story map on the next page.

"Chen! Chen, where are you?" called Lee. Only the October wind called back with great whooshing noises. Lee stood on a slippery rock that jutted up from the sea. She looked out across the water, but she couldn't see her brother or his boat. Lee was afraid.

The young girl had a small oil lamp and two matches from the boat. She blocked the wind with her body and tried to light the lamp. The first match sparked a little and then went dark. She hoped that the second match would light. She struck the match, and a small flame bloomed. Lee leaned toward the lamp, but a blast of wind stole her fire.

Then, Lee remembered the whistle her father gave her. She pulled it from her pocket and put it to her lips. Lee blew with all her might. The shriek of the whistle pushed against the wind. She blew again and the whistle sounded even louder. As she tried to blow once more, a large wave crashed into the rocks and knocked Lee into the sea. She swam to the rocks again, but her whistle was gone.

Lee was scared. The storm had taken her matches and her whistle. She tried calling her brother's name.

"Chen!" She waited and listened to the wind. "Chen!" Suddenly, Lee felt small and helpless. She sat down on the rocks and hid her face in her arms. Her body shook as she cried.

She lifted her head to wipe her tears, and a small light blinked at her. She looked again, but couldn't see anything. Lee stood up. A light out in the sea blinked. The waves bobbed up and down, and the light blinked with the waves. Her heart began to pound for joy. The light was coming from her brother's lamp. His boat had made it through the storm. Lee began to shout again. After a moment, she heard Chen's voice calling her name. Lee knew at last that all was well.

story structure   Name _____

***

Complete the story map below by writing the setting, characters, problem, events, and solution for the story on page 70.

1. Setting

    when _____

    where _____

2. Characters

    _____
    _____
    _____
    _____

3. Main Character's Problem

    _____
    _____
    _____
    _____
    _____
    _____

***

Events: What happens to keep the main character from getting what she wants?
Solution: How is the main character's problem resolved?

4. First,   (event)

    _____
    _____
    _____
    _____
    _____

5. Next,   (event)

    _____
    _____
    _____
    _____
    _____

6. Then,   (event)

    _____
    _____
    _____
    _____
    _____

7. Finally,   (solution)

    _____
    _____
    _____
    _____
    _____

Published by Instructional Fair. Copyright protected.   IF87134 *Building Writing Skills*

point of view · Name _____

Look at It This Way

The **point of view** shows who is telling the story.
• If a character tells the story, it is written in **first person**. The character will use the word "I" when telling the story.
 example: I rode as long as I could that day.
• A **narrator** is not a character in a story. The narrator will use words like he or she when telling the story.
 example: He rode as long as he could that day.
 example: Sally rode as long as she could that day.

Read each sentence below. Write **first person** or **narrator** on the line before the sentence. Then, rewrite the sentence from the other point of view.

1. _____ I crawled slowly down into the dark hole.
_____

2. _____ She jumped from one tree to the next like a squirrel.
_____

3. _____ I never wanted to see another bug in my life!
_____

4. _____ He wrote quickly, trying to finish before the buzzer.
_____

5. _____ Lord Bentley plays the game better than anyone.
_____

You're the author! Find a story that you like. Rewrite the story using a different point of view.

Published by Instructional Fair. Copyright protected. IF87134 Building Writing Skills

leads/hooks   Name _____

A Million Questions

A **lead** or a **hook** is the very beginning of a story. A good lead makes the reader ask questions. The reader wants to read the rest of the story to find out the answers. Here are three examples:

setting: The wind screamed as it tore across the city.

character: "I'll never do that again!" exclaimed Shanice.

action: She clung to the rope, hoping it wouldn't break.

Read the beginning of each story. Circle the letter of the best lead. Remember that a lead must interest the reader.

1. a. I heard it again last night.

   b. There was a noise.

   It sounded like the soft tapping of a branch on a window. The noise was quiet, but seemed as though it wanted to be heard—or needed to be heard.

2. a. The game ended.

   b. The final whistle blew, and it was all over.

   No one had thought Poncho's team was good enough to play in the final game. But now that they had won this game, everything had changed.

3. a. "Smoke! I see smoke," cried Li.

   b. Li saw smoke in the field.

   A trail of black reached up to touch the sky. Li and Ani watched silently. They both wondered how far away the fire was, and how fast it was moving.

4. a. The snow buried us in our house.

   b. There was a lot of snow.

   Uncle Oslo tried to push the door open. It was no use. We could see only white out the windows, but the strangest part was the silence.

Write your own lead for the beginning of this story.

5. _____

The small dog, named Foxy, ran to the window to see. Foxy jumped and barked until she heard the key in the door. She dashed to the front hall.

Check it out! Look for leads in the beginning of three good stories. What is it in each one that makes you want to keep reading?

story transitions   Name _____

Mrs. Reid's Vase

Transitions help the reader follow a story. They can show the order of things. They can also show how different ideas are connected. Story transitions often show a change in time or action. The transition words below are in bold.

Suddenly, the sky released the cold, wet rain in fat drops of water. The girls had to finish their game **later that day**. **While they were playing**, they heard the siren.

Detective Klause asked how Mrs. Reid's vase was broken. Read everyone's statement on the slips of paper below. Help Detective Klause put the story in order. Use the transitions to help you.

- When the lights came back on, the vase was broken.
- While it was dark, Khalil heard a cat screech and jump onto the table.
- While they were eating, Miguel tapped his fork against it to see if it was glass.
- Suddenly, lightning flashed outside, and the room went black.
- Before dinner, Janet picked up the vase to look at it.

Mrs. Reid's favorite vase was broken last night at dinner. _____

_____
_____
_____
_____
_____
_____

descriptions

The County Fair

A writer can use the five senses to describe things in a story. Look at the examples below.

see: The rocket left a white trail in the pink morning sky.
hear: The bells rang out with a clear, happy tune.
feel: The kitten was as soft as a rose petal.
taste: "Lemons taste so sour," she thought as her lips puckered.
smell: The scent of bacon and biscuits drifted through the camp.

Read each description. Color the numbered parts of the picture the right color for each sense. The key below shows what colors to use.

**see = blue   hear = red   feel = yellow   taste = orange
smell = green**

1. The buttery smell of popcorn drifts on the air.
2. Children's laughter is all around us.
3. Brightly colored lights dazzle our eyes.
4. The cheerful music from the rides sings to us.
5. Sweet, tangy taffy makes our mouths water.
6. The sun feels hot on our skin.
7. The balloon man sells red, green, purple, and yellow balloons.
8. I can smell hamburgers cooking on the grill.
9. The pretzels taste salty.

show, don't tell   Name _____

What the Reader Sees

Good writing allows the reader to see something in his or her mind. When writing, **don't tell** the reader about what is happening; **show** the reader. Use words to paint a picture for the reader to see.

tell: The meadow was pretty.

show: The alpine meadow glittered with the early morning dew. Tiny, white wildflowers bloomed among the meadow grass. The air was cool.

Circle the letter of the sentence that shows the reader a picture.

1. a. Trey ran all the way back to the school.
   b. He went back to school.
   c. Trey bolted three blocks back to school.

2. a. The bees flew around Beth's head.
   b. Thirty bees buzzed around Beth's head.
   c. There were lots of bees near Beth.

3. a. She stomped her feet and screamed at me.
   b. She was mad at me.
   c. She got mad and yelled at me.

4. a. The player was dirty.
   b. The player had mud on his clothes.
   c. The player's clothes were crusted with black dirt.

5. a. Rebbie was happy for her father.
   b. Rebbie smiled proudly at her father.
   c. Rebbie felt very happy for her dad.

This sentence tells the reader something. Rewrite it to show the reader something.

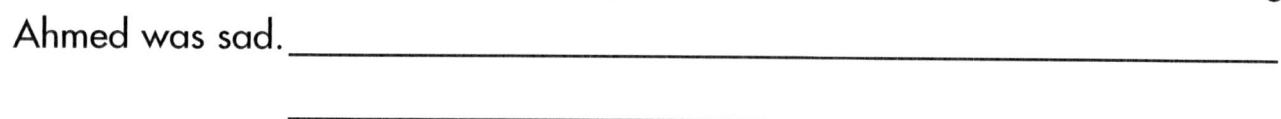

Ahmed was sad. _____

_____

You're the author! Write a setting. Paint your own picture with words.

action   Name _____

Show and Tell

Action makes stories interesting to read. When writing action in a story, remember to show, not tell. Make the reader feel he or she is there.

telling: He went back to the park. He found his gloves and went home.

showing: Worried that he had lost his new gloves, Josh ran back to the park where he had been playing a few hours ago. He searched the playground, but found nothing. He looked in the bushes. His gloves were not there. Josh sat on the bench, not knowing what he should do. Just then, a red-haired girl held out a pair of gloves and asked if they were his. Taking his gloves, Josh grinned, thanked the girl, and raced off for home.

Write **showing** or **telling** in front of each sentence.

1. _____ The children skipped down the long, dusty road.

2. _____ He went to a friend's house. They played computer games.

3. _____ Dad got out the rusty, old mower. He mowed the tall, green grass carefully, hoping the ancient machine would not quit.

Turn this telling sentence into a showing paragraph: It was a great party.

4. _____
_____
_____
_____
_____
_____
_____

You're the author! Write a showing story about a trip to Antarctica.

dialogue   Name _____

What's That, You Say?

Dialogue is simply characters talking with one another. Punctuation that shows the exact words being said are called **quotation marks**:

"**Hi, Josiah! Are you going to the class picnic?**" asked Aaron.
"**I wouldn't miss it,**" called Josiah.

Write the words from the characters' speech bubbles into the stories below.

1.

"_____?" asked Ben.
"_____," replied Waneka.
She felt nervous because she didn't know if Ben was invited to the party too.
"_____," said Ben.

2.

"_____?" called Uncle Hoot in his deep voice.
Milly stood on her hind legs. She said, "_____
_____."
"_____?" asked Uncle Hoot.

Published by Instructional Fair. Copyright protected.   IF87134 Building Writing Skills

quotation marks   Name _____

Snow Day!

Quotation marks show the character's exact words.

- Put quotations marks outside of the punctuation that is included in the quote.
- Capitalize the first word of the quote, unless the quote is the second part of a sentence.
- Separate a quotation from the rest of the sentence with a comma, question mark, or exclamation point.

"What does the news say about school?" asked Maya.
Her mother replied, **"No school today. It's a snow day!"**
"We will play a game," Dad said, **"after breakfast."**
Maya's brother wanted to know, **"Can we play in the snow?"**

Place quotation marks in these sentences.

1. You may play outside after you get dressed, said Mom.
2. Marco hollered from his room, Has anyone seen my gloves?
3. Look under your bed, said Mom, or maybe in the closet.
4. Are you going to build a snowman today? asked Dad.

Capitalize these sentences properly. Use the correct mark: s̲ue

5. maya exclaimed, "let's go! i'm ready!"
6. "you may go," said mom, "when marco is ready."

Punctuate the quotes in these sentences.

7. "Hey " said Maya "Don't throw snowballs at me "
8. "Did Marco throw it " asked Dad.
9. "It wasn't me Mom did it " laughed Marco.

Check it out! Find a story with dialogue. In the story, find one example of each type of quotation. Use the examples from the top of the page to help you.

Published by Instructional Fair. Copyright protected.   IF87134 Building Writing Skills

indenting quotes   Name _____

The Grand Wedding

Dialogue is written conversation. When a different character speaks, begin a new paragraph. Remember, new paragraphs are indented.

indented: "What brings you to town, my friend?" asked the good knight. He shook the farmer's hand.

indented: "I bring good news, Sir Hugh! My son is to be married," said the farmer. He smiled.

Rewrite this dialogue starting new paragraphs where needed. The first line is indented for you.

    The knight shouted, "Listen, everyone! My friend's son is to be married." "When is the day?" shouted the baker. "The week after we bring in the harvest. The whole town is invited!" said the farmer. "Hurray for the good farmer!" cheered the crowd.

_____
_____
_____
_____
_____
_____
_____
_____
_____
_____
_____

endings   Name _____

Fantastic Finishes

By the **end** of a story, the problem is solved. Sometimes the main character solves the problem. Sometimes the problem is solved in other ways. In a good ending, the author shows the solution to the reader.

Read each story and circle the letter for the best ending.

1. Scott scanned the ground for a place to land. Moni and Duk sat silently and looked out the windows. Thick trees spread as far as they could see. Only a thin break in the trees could be seen—the river.

    a. Scott pulled the plane into a sharp turn. He pushed on the throttle. The small plane dove to the straightest part of the river. With a loud crash, the plane slid safely onto the beach.

    b. As Scott pulled the plane into a turn, more smoke billowed from the engine. Moni gave a short gasp. The small plane jerked and bounced. With no open fields around, the river was their only hope.

2. A bitter cold swallowed the cabin. With no more firewood, it was hard to keep warm. The girls had burned the chairs and table. Even Lydia's books had gone into the fire. Now, as night closed in, the girls wondered how many more days they could last without heat.

    a. They pulled three blankets over themselves and hid under the covers at night. They shivered through the days, trying to say cheerful things. They were so cold.

    b. That night was as cold as ever. Even the cabin walls shook in the wind. But when they woke up in the morning, the sun was shining brightly. Some of the ice had melted. The cold spell was over.

You're the author! Write new endings for each of these stories. Remember to show the solution at the story's ending.

story titles   Name _____

It's All in the Name

The **title** is a very important part of a story. A title should give an idea of what the story is about but should not give away the ending. The title should make readers want to read the story.

The Million-Dollar Movie

A Flight to the Moons of Jupiter

The first word, the last word, and all important words in a title are capitalized. When book titles are printed in books or articles, they are in italics, *like this*. When you write a book title, underline it.

In a book: *Where the Wild Things Are*
When you write it: Where the Wild Things Are

Choose the best title for this story:

1. One night in the woods, I saw a bright, white spaceship land. I was scared, but I tried to be brave. I thought the aliens would ask me questions. They might even take me away to their planet. I decided I would run away. The spaceship opened, and my friend Paula got out. The spaceship was not a ship at all. It was just her family's camper.

    a. *The Ship*   b. *My Friend's Camper*   c. *A Spaceship in the Night*

Rewrite these book titles with correct capitalization. Be sure to underline them.

2. sarah, plain and tall _____
3. stone fox _____
4. the relatives came _____
5. number the stars _____
6. a light in the attic _____

Check it out! Find a book that you might like to read based on the title. Read the book. Did the title give you a hint about the story?

story elements

Tell Me a Story

Story elements are the basic parts of a story.

Complete the story-elements puzzle, using the clues and the Word Bank.

Word Bank

transitions
events
lead
point of view
solution
beginning
middle
end
dialogue
setting
characters
title
problem

Across
4. attempts to solve the problem
8. words used to show the order of events
11. people, animals, or things that do or say something in a story
12. how a story starts
13. the last part of a story

Down
1. where and when a story takes place
2. hooking the reader
3. shows who is telling the story
5. the name of the story
6. what the main character needs to solve
7. the body of the story
9. how the problem is solved
10. characters talking in a story

onomatopoeia   Name _____

Crash! Bang! Boom!

Onomatopoeia is the use of words that sound like the noises they represent. Using these words can make writing more interesting to read.

The machine **clicked** and **whirred**, but it still didn't work.
My mother's favorite dish fell to the floor with a **crash**!

Match the sounds to the animals or things that make the sounds.

a.

b.

c.

d.

e.

1. ring-ring ____
2. meow ____
3. tick-tock ____
4. flutter ____
5. quack ____
6. boom ____
7. woof ____
8. splash ____
9. boing ____
10. achoo ____

f.

g.

h.

i.

j.

You're the author! Write a short story with ten examples of onomatopoeia. Have fun!

alliteration and assonance   Name _____

Silly Safari Animals

Alliteration is a consonant sound repeated.

    On a **s**illy **s**afari, you **s**ee **s**inging **s**nakes.

    Li**tt**le **t**igers a**tt**ack big **t**igers' **t**ails.

Assonance is a vowel sound repeated. Remember that vowels can make more than one sound.

    African **a**nimals **a**lways **a**rgue with **a**lligators.

    Elegant **e**lephants **e**at **e**ggs.

Circle the repeating sounds and write **alliteration** or **assonance** on the line before each sentence.

1. _____ Lazy lions lie on the lawn.
2. _____ Zippy zebras zig-zag through the rocks.
3. _____ Old hippos get lonely only when they are alone.
4. _____ Each eagle has a sharp beak and strong feet.
5. _____ Grumpy gazelles gallop in groups.

6. _____ Odd otters hop on rocks.
7. _____ Ugly bugs hum while eating grubs.
8. _____ Jumbo jaguars jump and juggle.
9. _____ Funny fish flap their fins and flip.
10. _____ The wistful wildebeest wallowed in the water.

You're the author! Write ten sentences using alliteration and assonance.

similes

Just Like That

A **simile** compares two things using the words **like** or **as**. In writing, comparing things can make your meaning clearer.

Major Garcia had a voice **like a cannon**.

My sister is as gentle **as a lamb**.

Use the Word Bank to complete these similes.

	Word Bank	
quick	hot	stubborn
grown	runs	cold
sing	quiet	sank

1. Ms. Pazzi is as _____ as a mouse.
2. That soup is as _____ as the sun.
3. Ollie left as _____ as a flash.
4. A cheetah _____ like the wind.
5. My brother is as _____ as a mule.
6. Chung's brother has _____ like a weed.
7. The boat I made _____ like a rock.
8. This room is as _____ as ice.
9. Mrs. Robbins can _____ like a canary.

Write your own similes for these sentences.

10. Tabatha is _____
11. This truck is _____

personification

The Angry River

Giving human traits to an animal or a thing is called **personification**. A human trait is something people can do or be.

examples: The mice **talked** about how to stop the cat.
The mountain **stood** tall and **proud**.
Anger sat on his brow.

Read these sentences. Underline all the human traits.

1. A sudden wind teased the river.
2. The angry river beat on the rocks and shouted.
3. The roaring water frightened a lonely boat.
4. Waves stood tall and tossed the canoe.
5. The sad boat swam toward the shore.
6. Rocks bit into the side of the little boat.
7. The boat groaned with pain.
8. The storm grew tired and went to sleep.
9. The waves lay back down in the river.
10. The canoe limped to the shore and hugged the land.

Rewrite these sentences. Give the animals or objects human traits.

11. Rocks stuck out of the water. _____

12. The mouse made a nest. _____

13. The blue car went down the street. _____

choosing a topic Name _____

What Shall I Write?

What shall I write? To answer this question, a writer must know the reason, or **purpose** for writing. The writer must also know who the readers, or **audience**, will be.

Read the description of the audience and purpose. Then, choose the best topic to match the audience and purpose.

1. **Audience:** your teacher and classmates
   Purpose: give information about whales

   a. "The Whale in Pinocchio"

   b. "The Life Cycle of Whales"

   c. "The Whale I Saw Last Year"

2. **Audience:** a visiting Japanese baseball team
   Purpose: talk about a time you played baseball

   a. "The Day I Stole Third Base"

   b. "The History of Baseball"

   c. "The Best Team in Japan"

Choose the best audience for these topics.

3. Topic: "How to Build a Campfire"

   a. a Boy Scout Troop   b. a quilting club

4. Topic: "The Talking Cat"

   a. the city police department   b. a first-grade class

5. Topic: "The Most Beautiful Sunset"

   a. art teachers   b. the soccer club

Write your own topics for these audiences.

6. the President of the United States _____

7. the teachers at your school _____

Published by Instructional Fair. Copyright protected.   88   IF87134 Building Writing Skills

prompts   Name _____

Prompt Me

A **prompt** is an idea for writing. Sometimes a writer is asked to write to a prompt. It is important to know what is being asked and what type of writing is required.

    Expository writing gives information or explains something.
    Narrative writing tells a story.

Write **expository** or **narrative** on the line before the prompt to tell which type of writing is required.

1. _____ Write a story about life on a farm.

2. _____ Write a page to tell your class how to make a kite. Remember to tell what materials they will need.

3. _____ Write a report that tells how rivers become polluted. Tell about the causes of the pollution and the effects on the river animals.

4. _____ Write about two women who live on Mars. Invent the tools and buildings they need to live.

5. _____ Pretend that you want a pet parrot. Write a paper to talk your parents into letting you have one. Use three reasons to help persuade them.

6. _____ Describe your favorite toy. Explain what it looks like and what you like to do with it. Share your report with the class. Can they guess your favorite toy?

7. _____ Compare and contrast your favorite game with a game you do not like. Then, explain why you like one but not the other.

8. _____ Tell a story about a brother and sister that get in trouble for their silly jokes. Describe one of their jokes and tell how they get caught.

planning expository writing   Name _____

What a Plan!

Expository writing gives information or explains something. Before writing an expository piece, plan what you will write. **Plans** are used to put ideas in order. Write out topic sentences and concluding sentences completely in your plan. Other parts of the plan do not need to be written in complete sentences.

Choose the words or sentences from the list below to write into your plan. The transition words are written to help you.

   a. First, they eat insects.
   b. females are stronger than males
   c. The black widow spider seems strange and scary to me.
   d. Last, the female spiders can bite people.
   e. black widow spiders do not bite if left alone
   f. they will not eat plants; pet owner has to find live food
   g. Second, the female spiders sometimes eat the males.
   h. All these are reasons why I would not want a black widow for a pet.

1. topic sentence: _____
   _____

2. a. first idea: _____
   b. tell more: _____

3. a. second idea: _____
   b. tell more: _____

4. a. third idea: _____
   b. tell more: _____

5. concluding sentence: _____
   _____

You're the author! Write a paragraph from your black widow spider expository plan.

description planning   Name _____

My Dream Truck

One type of expository writing is **description**. Describing an object is easy with a plan. Ideas can be written in a web like this one. All of the thoughts in the outer circles tell about a dream truck.

- deep metallic blue
- chrome wheels
- my dream truck
- huge tires
- silver stripes
- cool stereo

Write the ideas from the web into the plan. Put connected ideas together. There are only five ideas listed, so add one of your own connected ideas.

1. topic sentence: It has always been my dream to own a pickup truck.
2. a. one idea: _____
   b. connected idea: _____
3. a. another idea: _____
   b. connected idea: _____
4. a. last idea: _____
   b. connected idea: _____
5. concluding sentence: When I grow up, I plan to buy a truck just like this!
6. Write three ideas about this description: My dream vacation.
   a. first idea _____
   b. second idea: _____
   c. third idea: _____

You're the author! Make a plan and write about your own dream car.

narrative planning   Name _____

A Treasure Map

Narrative writing tells a story. To plan a story, use a story map.

Plan a story using the story map and ideas given. Write the ideas in the plan.

a. We find a bottle with a treasure map inside, but we don't know if it's real or not.

b. Finally, we follow the map ourselves and find the treasure.

c. Second, we search for clues on the dock, but we don't find any.

d. my best friend and me

e. at the beach, on Saturday

f. Next, we ask the captain of a boat, but he can't remember where the map came from.

g. First, we ask our parents if the map is real; they don't know.

1. a. setting: _____
    b. characters: _____
    c. problem: _____
    _____

2. first event: _____
    _____

3. second event: _____
    _____

4. third event: _____
    _____

5. solution: _____
    _____

You're the author! Write a story about a treasure map, using the plan.

staying on topic

The Moon

Staying on topic helps the reader to follow the writer's ideas. Information that is not on topic should be removed. This is one way to revise, or make your writing better.

topic: Rocks from the moon
on topic: Astronauts brought rocks back from the moon.
off topic: In first grade, I wanted to go to the moon.

Read each report. Cross out the sentences or paragraphs that are not on topic.

Rocks on the Moon

Astronauts in 1969 brought rocks back from the moon. When the rocks were brought back to earth, people studied them. They learned many things about the moon.

I would love to study the rocks from the moon. I want to be an astronaut. I'd like to fly to Mars and study the rocks there too.

One of the things the people learned from studying the rocks is the age of the moon. The moon is about 4.2 billion years old. The rocks also told us that there is very little water on the moon. I wonder what the astronauts drank on their trip.

A Race to the Moon

In the 1960s, there was a race to get to the moon. The Americans and the Russians each wanted to be the first to land on the moon. I wonder what it was like to watch that race.

The Russians started the race by launching a rocket into space. They took the lead in the race to the moon. The moon is very old.

Then, in 1969, the United States sent up a spaceship that landed on the moon. Three men went on that journey. My dad watched it on TV. When Neil Armstrong stepped onto the surface of the moon, the Americans had won the race at last.

extraneous information

Is That Your Mummy?

When improving your writing, or **revising**, it is important to read everything that is written. Then, cut out words and sentences that are not needed.

Read the sentences and cross out the words that are not needed.

1. Everyone knows there are mummies in Egypt in pyramids.
2. Also, mummies can be found in other countries, too.
3. The most famous mummy is an Egyptian king from Egypt.
4. Mummies are very old and from a long time ago.

Rewrite the following sentence. Take out the words that are not needed.

5. Mummies were buried with treasure and gold and gems and jewels.

_____

_____

Read the paragraph and cross out the sentences that are not needed.

6. Riches, furniture, and personal items are often found in mummies' tombs. Egyptian kings were buried with gold and jewels. Gold vases and pitchers were also common burial items. Gold workers made beautiful art. Sometimes, mummies had chairs or beds in their burial chambers. Tables were set up with figs and bread. After 3,000 years, the figs are too hard to eat now. Almost all mummies are found with some personal things, even if they were not rich. Female mummies were buried with fans and mirrors. Child mummies are found with toys. Male mummies were buried with their tools. Mummies had all these things in their tombs to take with them to the afterlife. I like reading about mummies.

elaboration

Name _____

A New Planet

After writing, go back to **revise**, or make your writing better. One way to do this is to add examples, explanations, or descriptions.

no example: Astronauts do brave things.

example: Astronauts do brave things like fly to new planets.

no explanation: The crew hid in the cave.

explanation: The crew hid in the cave to get out of the sandstorm.

no description: The ground was weird.

description: The ground was a soft red, with millions of tiny holes.

Choose the right letter to revise the underlined words in the sentence. A hint after each sentence tells what kind of detail to add.

1. The clouds <u>were strange</u>. (give an example)

    a. looked like huge, flat stones floating in the sky.

    b. were scary-looking.

2. The astronauts wore <u>shiny suits</u>. (explain)

    a. shiny suits with flags and emblems.

    b. shiny suits to protect them from the heat and cold.

3. <u>Rocks</u> jutted out of the ground. (add description)

    a. Different kinds of stones

    b. Jagged, black rocks

4. No plants <u>grow here</u>. (explain)

    a. bloom and thrive here.

    b. can grow here because there is no water.

You're the author! Rewrite the four sentences above to add more detail.

specific writing   Name _____

That's Clear

Specific words tell the reader more than vague or unclear words.

                The bubble broke.
vivid verb: The bubble **burst**.

                The teacher cried when she read the book.
added names: **Mrs. Brenner** cried when she read *The Invisible Man*.

                He saw something in the water.
specific word: He saw a **jellyfish** in the water.

Read each sentence. Then choose the revised sentence that makes it clearer. A hint after each sentence will tell what kind of specific word is needed.

1. He stood by the fire and looked out at the snow. (name)

   a. The old man stood by the fire and looked out at the new snow.

   b. Old Mr. Janski stood by the fire and looked out at the new snow.

2. My friend broke the mirror in the bathroom. (vivid verb)

   a. Someone broke the bathroom mirror.

   b. My friend shattered the mirror in the bathroom.

3. The thief left some stuff in the safe. (specific word)

   a. The thief left some valuables in the safe.

   b. The thief left some diamonds in the safe.

4. A scientist looked through the microscope. (name and specific words)

   a. Dr. Singh, the famous chemist, looked through the microscope.

   b. The scientist looked through the old microscope.

You're the author! Write a story, or use one you wrote at another time. Revise your writing by changing boring, vague words into specific words.

Published by Instructional Fair. Copyright protected.   IF87134 *Building Writing Skills*

unclear references

Swamp Water

Each pronoun in a sentence takes the place of a specific noun. If the reader cannot tell which noun goes with the pronoun, the sentence can be confusing. The sentence must be revised to make the meaning clear.

He looked at the maps and the book and saw that **they** were wet.
unclear: Does **they** mean the maps or the maps and the book?
He looked at the maps and the book. The maps were wet.
clear: Only the maps were wet.

Read each sentence. Write down the noun or nouns that go with the pronoun.

1. Old Jacques asked Maria if she wanted a ride in the swamp boat.
   What noun goes with she? _____

2. He took her to see an old tree. It was the giant of the swamp.
   What noun goes with it? _____

3. One Fang, a big alligator, swam past the boat. He was silent.
   What noun goes with he? _____

4. Maria looked at Jacques and said that she was afraid.
   What noun goes with she? _____

5. When Jacques and Maria got back, he offered to catch some fish for her.
   What noun goes with he? _____

The pronoun in this sentence is confusing. Rewrite the sentence to make it clear.

6. The swamp rat scared Maria and Jacques, but he jumped into the water.

   _____
   _____
   _____

revising fragments

Vesuvius

A complete sentence has a subject and a predicate, and is a complete thought. A **fragment** is missing one or more of these.

sentence: Vesuvius is a volcano in Italy.

fragment: A volcano in Italy.

When revising, check to make sure all sentences are complete sentences. Rewrite fragments so they are complete sentences.

Read the paragraph. Underline the **fragments**, and rewrite them as complete sentences at the bottom of the page.

Vesuvius

Vesuvius is the name of a volcano in Italy. A very famous volcano. It is the volcano that erupted and buried a whole city with ash. The market city, Pompeii. Vesuvius has erupted more than ten times since it buried Pompeii. Some of the eruptions are very small. Some are very large. Like the time it buried Pompeii. Today, people watch Vesuvius closely. Because the volcano is still so dangerous.

1. _____
_____
2. _____
_____
3. _____
_____
4. _____
_____

varying sentences   Name _____

Too Many Little Ones

When a writer uses the same kind of sentence over and over, the reader can get bored. Changing the length and type of sentence makes what you write more fun to read.

Read the sentences. Combine each pair to make one longer sentence.

1. There are elves in my uncle's attic. There are more than twenty elves.
   _____

2. The elves make a lot of noise. The elves stay up all night.
   _____

3. Elves play in the kitchen. They play in the music room.
   _____

This paragraph has too many short sentences. Rewrite the paragraph to make some of the sentences longer.

    The elves in my uncle's attic like to have fun. The elves wear tiny green hats. They have small pants. They have small shirts. The elves like to dance. The elves like to sing. When the elves have fun, no one can sleep.

_____
_____
_____
_____
_____
_____

editing verbs   Name _____

Fishing with My Grandfather

Editing means checking your writing to find errors. One type of error is using the wrong form of a verb. This could mean that the verb does not agree with the subject. It could also mean that the verb is in the wrong tense. The verb tense tells whether the action happens in the past, present, or future.

Read the paragraph below. Decide whether or not each underlined verb form is correct. If not, decide what the correct form should be. Circle the correct choice.

Last year, my grandfather <u>takes</u> me to his secret fishing hole. We woke up
                                      1
early in the morning. I carried the tackle box and he <u>will carry</u> the poles. We
                                                                 2
<u>followed</u> a trail for a little while, but then we <u>are leaving</u> the path. He led me
   3   4
over a hill. Then, we <u>crosses</u> a log bridge. Soon we <u>were standing</u> at the edge of
                           5   6
a small lake. My grandfather <u>will put</u> a worm on the hook for me. We <u>catched</u>
                                     7   8
five big fish on that day. The best part of our fishing trip was that I got to spend time with my grandfather.

1. a. took
   b. take
   c. no error

2. a. is carrying
   b. carried
   c. no error

3. a. follows
   b. will follow
   c. no error

4. a. leaves
   b. left
   c. no error

5. a. are crossing
   b. crossed
   c. no error

6. a. stand
   b. stands
   c. no error

7. a. put
   b. did put
   c. no error

8. a. caught
   b. catches
   c. no error

editing spelling

Apples for Everyone

Editing means checking your writing to find errors. One type of error is incorrect spelling.

Read the paragraphs below. Circle the five misspelled words in each paragraph. Then, write the corrected words on the lines.

Apple Picking

I love autumn when the leaves start to change colors. It is a special time for my famile. My mom always takes us up to the mountains where we get to pick the biggest, juiciest apples. After we pick the apples, we stop to have a peece of hot apple pie. When we get home, we make some apple treats for are autumn party. All of our very best freinds come to celebrate with us. That's why autumn means so much to me.

1. _____
2. _____
3. _____
4. _____
5. _____

Addie's Apple Adventure

It happend five years ago. Addie had just finished picking a basket of apples. She was walking home threw the woods. Suddenly, an old crow swooped out of the sky and swiped one of the apples. When the crow gave a loud cry, more crows came. Thay flew down and grabbed the apples. Addie dropped the basket and ran. The hole town saw Addie runing after a long line of crows. Every crow had one of Addie's apples.

6. _____
7. _____
8. _____
9. _____
10. _____

editing punctuation   Name _____

The Great Horse Escape

Editing means checking your writing to find errors. One type of error is incorrect punctuation. Some common mistakes are forgetting to use **end marks**, **quotation marks**, and **commas in a series**.

Read the paragraphs below. Decide which kind of error is shown in each underlined section. Mark your answer below.

Three horses lived in a old, red barn. Their names were (1) <u>Jumper Twigs and Ashe</u>. During a storm on a hot summer night, a flash of lightning started a fire on the roof of the barn. Flames gobbled up the old, dry wood. The horses pulled against their ropes. (2) <u>They couldn't break free</u>

(3) <u>Help! Help!</u> called Jumper.

Whiskers, the river rat, climbed up to the ropes. "I will chew through your ropes if you promise to always give me some (4) <u>of your food</u>" said the rat. The horses all promised. Whiskers chewed through the ropes. The horses (5) <u>jumped out of their stalls ran to the end of the barn and kicked open the doors</u>. To this day, the farmers don't know how the horses made their great escape.

1. a. missing commas in a series
   b. missing quotation marks
   c. missing end mark

2. a. missing commas in a series
   b. missing quotation marks
   c. missing end mark

3. a. missing commas in a series
   b. missing quotation marks
   c. missing end mark

4. a. missing commas in a series
   b. missing quotation marks
   c. missing end mark

5. a. missing commas in a series
   b. missing quotation marks
   c. missing end mark

editing capitalization

Name _____

Awful Ads

When **editing** a piece of writing, check for proper capitalization. The editing mark for capitalization looks like three underlines.

beginning of a sentence: the best deals in town are here.
proper noun titles: Shouldn't you try jake's rib house?
titles: Pick up your copy of *charlotte's web*.
inside quotation marks: Everyone says, "there's no better place."

Read the ads. Add the editing mark for capitalization when a letter should be capitalized. Remember to capitalize the beginning of each sentence, proper nouns, titles, and the first word of a sentence inside quotation marks.

Carol's Crunchy Cookies

these are the best cookies in town. If you try them once, you will come back for more. one customer said, "i want to eat them all day." Come in and try some cookies today!

the auto place

Nowhere in town can you find more cars. We have the best deal on the car you need. now, when you buy a car from us, we will give you a copy of the book, *amazing automobiles*. Hurry in today!

Booker's Book Shop

Are you looking for a copy of *treasure island*? Do you want to read *the lorax*? come in to Booker's book Shop. We promise that we have the book you want. Mr. kahn says, "there is no book shop like booker's." at Booker's, we will keep you reading.

editing paragraphing   Name _____

Messy Monsters

The editing mark to show where a **new paragraph** should begin looks like this: ¶

Begin a paragraph whenever there is a new main idea or whenever a different character speaks. Remember that transition words can show where a new idea begins.

Makaela wrote a story. Help her edit her work. Place the paragraph editing marks where she forgot to start the new paragraphs.

A little girl named Rose had a problem with monsters. Every night while she slept, the monsters crept from their hiding places and played with her toys. The real problem was that they never cleaned up after they were done. When Rose's mother came to get Rose up in the morning, the room was always a mess. Rose did not know what to do. One night, she tried to trick the monsters. Rose took all her toys out of her toy chest. She put them in her closet and closed the door. In the morning, her room was a mess again. The monsters had found the toys. The next night, Rose left a plate of cookies in the middle of the room. She thought the monsters would eat the cookies and forget about the toys. The monsters did enjoy the cookies, but they also enjoyed the toys. Finally, Rose ran out of ideas. No matter what she tried, the monsters kept playing with her toys and then leaving a mess. "Write a note to remind yourself to clean up your room," said her mother. "I didn't make the mess, Mom," said Rose. "The mess is in your room," said her mom, "so you have to clean it up. That's the rule." Rose sighed. She went to her room and got out a pencil and paper. She wrote a note to ask the monsters to please clean up their mess. Rose said in her note that if the monsters wanted to play in her room, they had to clean up when they were done; even monsters had to follow the rules! The next morning Rose woke up to her mom's smiling face and her words of thanks for Rose's nice, clean room.

short answers

Favorite Fairy Tales

When writing an answer to a question, always answer in a complete sentence. Use the question words in the answer.

question: How long did **Sleeping Beauty sleep**?
answer: **Sleeping Beauty slept** for a hundred years.
question: What type of house did **the first little pig build**?
answer: **The first little pig built** a house out of straw.

Use the question words to write your answers in complete sentences.

1. Whose house did Goldilocks visit? _____

2. Where was Little Red Riding Hood going? _____

3. Who tried to blow down the houses of the Three Little Pigs? _____

4. What type of shoes did Cinderella wear? _____

5. Who fell in love with Beauty? _____

6. When did Cinderella leave the ball? _____

7. What happened to Pinocchio's nose when he lied? _____

8. How do most fairy tales end? _____

short answers   Name _____

The Odd Octopus

Short answers should be written in complete sentences. They need to be supported with details from the text. Use at least **two details** from the text to support your answer.

Example question: What makes a good short answer?

Example answer: A good short answer is a complete sentence supported with at least two details from the text.

Read each paragraph and question. Choose the best short answer.

1.   An octopus is a strange animal. First, an octopus has no bones. Because of this, an octopus can fit into very small places. Also, in order to hide, an octopus can change the color of its skin. Finally, an octopus swims by pushing water out of its body in the same way a jet engine works. An octopus is truly a unique animal.

   How is an octopus different from many other animals?

   a. An octopus doesn't have bones.

   b. An octopus is different because it has no bones, and it can change colors.

   c. An octopus can fit into very small places.

   d. An octopus is a strange animal because it swims like a jet engine.

2.   A little octopus named Oscar lived in a small cave at the bottom of a beautiful blue sea. One day, Oscar was looking for something to eat when he saw a strange object. He took a closer look. He found a small opening on one end and a big space in the middle, just like his cave. When Oscar squeezed in, he could see through the walls to the outside. There was an odd pattern on the side of the cave that looked like this: COLA. Oscar didn't mind the strange pattern. He liked his new home.

   What did Oscar's new home look like?

   a. Oscar's new home was a cola bottle.

   b. Oscar's new home looked like a rocky cave.

   c. Oscar's new home had a small opening and the word COLA on it.

Published by Instructional Fair. Copyright protected.   106   IF87134 *Building Writing Skills*

summaries   Name _____

What's the Point?

A **summary** is a **short version** of a paragraph, book, or story. A one-sentence summary tells the title and author as well as the theme. The **theme** is the **point** or **overall message** of the book.

Examples:

The Little Engine That Could by Watty Piper reveals what can be done when you believe in yourself.

Charlotte's Web by E. B. White shows the power of friendship.

Read each selection. Choose the best theme for each selection.

1. The new girl sat in the cafeteria, all alone. Everyone joked about the way she talked. I remembered the way I felt when I was the new girl. No one would talk to me, either. That's why I sat next to her. I found out that she is still learning English, but she speaks Spanish very well. Wow! I only know one language! She's going to come to my house on Friday to teach me how to play some games from her country.

    This story shows that

    a. learning a new language is important.

    b. you should treat others the way you would like to be treated.

2. We were one run away from winning the championship, and it was Randy's turn at bat—Randy, who only had two hits all season. Our star player, Ang, sat on the bench and sulked. The rest of us cheered for Randy. "Strike one!" We told Randy he could do it. "Strike two!" We shouted even louder. Then the bat cracked against the ball. The ball seemed to float into the outfield. Sheila ran home from third base, and we won! Even Ang was cheering. Randy was the hero of the game!

    This story shows that

    a. everyone on a team is important.

    b. the best players should be the heroes.

You're the author! Write a one-sentence summary of your favorite story. Don't forget to include the name of the story and who wrote it.

Published by Instructional Fair. Copyright protected.   IF87134 *Building Writing Skills*

summaries   Name _____

The Lost City

To **summarize narrative writing**, or stories, include some of these story elements: setting, characters, problem, events, and solution.

Read the story passage. Then, choose the best summary. Remember that the summary should include some of the basic story elements.

1.   The light from the campfire pushed back the night. Lester and Jayla worked in the glow. When they first wandered into the lost city, they were thrilled. Now that it was time to leave, they needed a map so they could find the city again. They had no blank paper or pens in their packs. Lester tried to make some ink to write on bark, but it didn't work. Jayla pulled out her pocket knife and began to carve on a piece of wood. As the fire burned, the two adventurers carved their map. They would be back.

    a. Lester and Jayla get lost in the woods.
    b. Two friends find a map that leads to a lost city.
    c. Two friends named Lester and Jayla try different ways to make a map so they can return to a lost city.

Write your own summary for this earlier part of the story.

2.   While they were exploring one of the buildings in the lost city, a wall crashed to the ground. None of the large stones struck the two, but a small, sharp rock hit Jayla's leg. She slumped down on an old tree trunk. Lester looked in his pack for a bandage, but he didn't have one. He poured some drinking water on the cuts and cleaned them. Lester wanted to use a piece of clothing to wrap around the wound, but their clothes were too dirty. Finally, he found some long, oval leaves to wind around Jayla's leg. Then Lester was able to help her back to their camp.

_____
_____
_____

book reports

Mean Sam Clemm

A **book report** gives information about the book or story. It also offers an opinion of the book.

Read the story. Then complete the report about it. For question 5, circle the words "liked" or "didn't like," and then use your own words to tell how you felt about the story.

Sam Clemm grumbled about everything. He was a big man with a bushy beard and squinting, black eyes. One day Sam rode his horse to town to go to the bank. He tied his horse to the rail and went through the doors. When he came out, a little girl in a pink dress was looking at his horse. Then she touched the horse's leg gently.

"What are you doing?" hollered the grumpy man.

The little girl looked as if she was going to cry. She was so scared that she couldn't look at Sam. Instead, she pointed a tiny finger at the brown markings on the horse's leg.

"What about my horse?" cried Sam again. He was losing patience.

"This," whispered the girl, pointing, "looks like a big smile and two eyes."

"What?" asked Sam, confused. He looked at the markings.

"It makes me happy," said the girl. "Doesn't it make you happy to ride a smiley horse?"

Sam tilted his head and squinted at his horse. Then he saw the pattern too. Sam smiled. "Yes," he said, "it does make me happy." Sam rode his smiley horse out of town, smiling as he went.

1. This story is about _____

2. In the story, Sam Clemm _____

3. When Sam is in the bank, the little girl _____

4. The best part of this story happens when _____
_____
_____

5. I liked/didn't like this story because _____
_____

taking notes   Name _____

Take Note of This

Taking notes helps people think about and remember the information that they read. When you take notes, you write down only the most important information from a passage. The first step in taking notes is finding the **main idea**.

Find the main idea for each paragraph.

1.   The sunny day slowly clouded over. The soft breeze changed suddenly into an icy wind. Large, dark, clouds formed over the mountains. Above our heads, the air became heavy with moisture. A bright flash over the mountains blinded our eyes for a moment. The flash was followed by a loud *kaboom*!

    a. The mountains looked pretty.

    b. The sun was bright.

    c. A storm was coming.

    d. Clouds were in the sky.

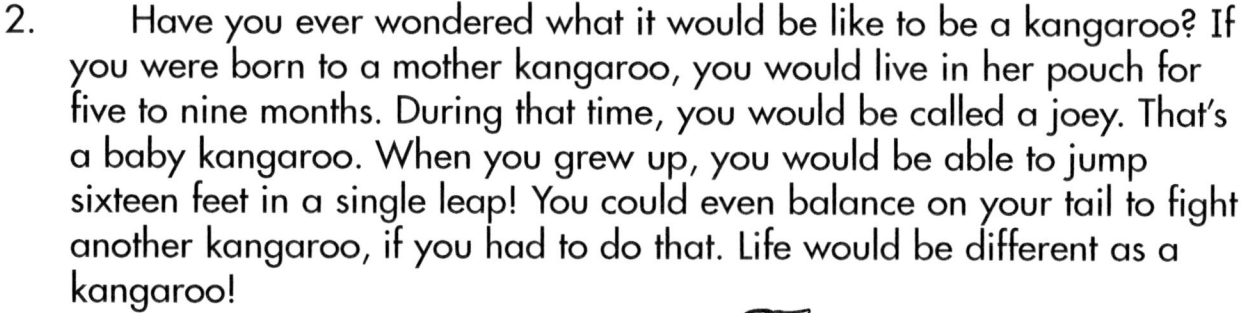

2.   Have you ever wondered what it would be like to be a kangaroo? If you were born to a mother kangaroo, you would live in her pouch for five to nine months. During that time, you would be called a joey. That's a baby kangaroo. When you grew up, you would be able to jump sixteen feet in a single leap! You could even balance on your tail to fight another kangaroo, if you had to do that. Life would be different as a kangaroo!

    a. baby kangaroos

    b. Australian kangaroos

    c. life as a kangaroo

    d. fighting kangaroos

taking notes   Name _____

Geysers of Yellowstone

Taking notes is writing down only the most important information. The first step in taking notes is finding the main idea. Then, write down the most important details.

Read the paragraphs. Complete the notes with main ideas and details from the text. Use the Idea Bank to help you.

The Geysers of Yellowstone

Yellowstone Park is known for its geysers. There are more than 300 geysers in the park. A geyser is formed when water is trapped under the ground. Melted rock, like lava, heats the water. When the water boils, it shoots through a hole in the ground. Water and steam shoot high into the air when a geyser erupts.

The best-known geyser is Old Faithful. Old Faithful erupts about every 75 minutes. It is as faithful as a clock. Old Faithful's eruptions can last up to five minutes. The steam and water shoot up to 184 feet (56m) in the air. There are bigger geysers in Yellowstone Park, but no other geyser is as famous as Old Faithful.

first paragraph

1. main idea: _____
   _____
2. detail: _____
3. detail: _____

second paragraph

4. main idea: _____
   _____
5. detail: _____
6. detail: _____

Idea Bank

Old Faithful is well known.

boiling water erupts

Yellowstone has many geysers.

it erupts on time

water shoots 184 feet (56m) in the air

melted rock heats water

Published by Instructional Fair. Copyright protected.   IF87134 *Building Writing Skills*

summarizing   Name _____

Harriet Tubman

A **summary** is a **short version** of a paragraph, book, or story. To write a summary, find the main ideas. Then, find the important details. From this information, write a summary.

Read the selection about Harriet Tubman. Main ideas and important details are underlined. Circle the letter of the best summary below based on these main ideas and details.

<u>Harriet Araminta Ross was born into slavery in about 1820 in the South.</u> She worked as a slave in the fields of a farm. She also worked as a house servant. <u>When she grew up, she married John Tubman, who was a free black man.</u>

<u>Harriet escaped slavery by running away to the North, or free states. Harriet became a free woman.</u> Even though she was free, she wanted to help other blacks escape to freedom. <u>She made many dangerous trips along the freedom trail to help others escape. She helped them by way of the Underground Railroad.</u> This was not a railroad at all. It was a secret system of safe places for slaves to hide. It was set up by people who believed everyone should be free. <u>She led about 300 other people to freedom.</u> Like Moses of ancient times, Harriet Tubman helped her people escape from slavery.

a. Harriet Tubman, a slave who became free, helped many other people escape slavery. She ran a train called the Underground Railroad.

b. Harriet Tubman was a slave. She got married to be free. She helped people on the Underground Railroad. It was not a railroad, but a way to help others reach freedom. Her new last name was Moses.

c. Harriet Ross was born a slave. She married a free man, John Tubman. Harriet became a free woman when she escaped to the North. She made many trips along the Underground Railroad to help guide about 300 other people to freedom.

d. Harriet Ross married John Tubman. Together they escaped slavery. They helped others escape from the Underground Railroad.

summarizing

The Exxon *Valdez*

A **summary** is a shortened version of a paragraph, book, or story. Newspaper articles are written with the most important information first. Use the same techniques newspapers use when writing a summary about an event. Include **who** or **what**, **did what**, **where**, **when**, and **why** in your summary.

Read the article. Underline the **who** or **what**, **did what**, **where**, **when**, and **why** in the article. Then circle the letter to choose the summary, which should include all of these important details.

Oil tankers are very large ships that carry oil. The Exxon *Valdez* is an oil tanker. On the night of March 24, 1989, the Exxon *Valdez* was in Prince William Sound, a bay in southern Alaska. The ship ran aground on Bligh Reef. Then oil in the ship began to leak.

The Exxon *Valdez* leaked for two days. It was the worst oil spill in United States history. The rest of the oil on the ship was moved to other ships, but horrible damage was done. Over eleven million barrels of oil polluted the water and shoreline. The oil hurt or killed thousands of birds and sea animals. Oil companies paid a lot of money to fix the problem—over two billion dollars. But nothing could bring back the lives of the birds, fish, and other animals that died in the oil spill.

a. On March 24, 1989, the Exxon *Valdez* ran aground and spilled oil. The oil leaked for two days. The spill killed many birds and animals.

b. The Exxon *Valdez* spilled oil after it ran aground on Bligh Reef in Alaska. The oil caused major pollution. Oil companies paid billions of dollars to clean up the oil.

c. The oil tanker, Exxon *Valdez*, spilled oil into Alaska's Prince William Sound on the night of March 24, 1989. It was the worst oil spill in U.S. history because over eleven million barrels of oil polluted the water, damaged the shoreline, and killed many birds and sea animals.

friendly letters   Name_____

Dear Grandma

A friendly letter has five different parts: a **heading**, a **greeting**, a **body**, a **closing**, and a **signature**. Each part has its own special place in a letter.

November 1, 2001

Dear Grandma,

   I miss you. I can't wait until you come for a visit. Do you want to play cards when you get here? My favorite is "Go Fish." Mom says we can eat turkey and stuffing when you come. What a celebration that will be! Hurry, Thanksgiving!

With love,

Kimmie

The **heading** of a friendly letter can include the sender's address and the date, or just the date. It starts halfway across the page.

The **greeting** of a letter is the hello. Often the word "Dear" is used with the name of the person to whom the letter is written. It starts on the left side.

The **body** of the letter is the main part of the letter. It is written in paragraphs.

The **closing** is the goodbye. It is usually a kind thought (With love) or a naming of the writer (Your grand-daughter). It lines up with the heading.

The **signature** is the writer's signed name. It appears directly beneath the closing, and lines up with it.

Use the words in bold above to help you fill in the blanks.

1. the letter writer's signed name_____
2. the sender's address and date_____
3. the "goodbye" of the letter _____
4. the part of the letter written in paragraphs _____
5. the "hello" of the letter _____
6. the parts that line up halfway across the page _____

Published by Instructional Fair. Copyright protected.   114   IF87134 Building Writing Skills

friendly letter   Name _____

Invitation

A **friendly letter** has five parts: a heading, a greeting, a body, a closing, and a signature. Each part has its own place in a letter.

Dates must be capitalized with a comma between the date and year:
October 18, 2001 or **March 14, 2002**

The **greeting and closing** should begin with capital letters. Any other words, except for names, start with lowercase letters. Both the greeting and closing are followed by a comma.
My dear friend, or **With my love,**

Rewrite the date, greeting, and closings correctly.

1. october 12 1492 _____
2. sincerely _____
3. my dear mr. claus _____
4. yours very Truly _____

The letter below was not written in the correct form. There are also some mistakes. Rewrite the letter correctly on the lines.

march 15 2002 dear Jeremy I wish you could play basketball on our team. We start practice on april 3. Can you join us? I hope so!
    your friend Olivia

_____
_____
_____
_____
_____
_____
_____
_____
_____
_____

addressing envelopes   Name _____

It's in the Mail

Addressing an envelope is the last step before sending a letter. Two addresses appear on an envelope. The **mailing address** tells who will receive the letter. The **return address** tells who is sending the letter.

An address includes a name, a number and street name, a city, a state, and a zip code. All words should be capitalized. A comma separates the city and the state.

      Mr. Oliver Sanchez
      1234 Silver Springs Drive
      Bangor, Maine 04401

Correct the errors in these addresses. Underline letters three times that should be capitalized. Add commas where they are needed.

1. mrs harriet colles
   845 pine street
   garnet montana 59770

2. shelby perkins
   3572 sunshine lane
   davies florida 32802

3. Write your own name and address below for the return address. Correct the punctuation and capitalization on the mailing address.

    nathaniel apayauk
    72 tundra road
    barrow alaska 99723

poetry

A Couple of Couplets

Poetry tells about feelings, ideas, or events, often with fewer words than regular writing. Some poems rhyme and some poems do not. A poem can be whatever the writer wants it to be. Poems do not need to have complete sentences.

A **couplet** is a pair of rhyming lines. Poems can be made by combining couplets. Line **a** rhymes with another line **a**, and line **b** rhymes with another line **b**.

Sometimes the rhymes are together, like this:

- **a** Carrots, beans, or peas?
- **a** Who wants to eat these?
- **b** I won't tell a lie.
- **b** We'd like cake and pie.

Sometimes the rhymes are apart, like this:

- **a** A timeless tree stood
- **b** on the edge of a dream,
- **a** and thought that he could
- **b** run like the stream.

Choose and write the correct word to complete each couplet.

1. **a** City noises, dirty air, crowded street.
   a Country sun, soaring birds, rows of_____.

   i. corn   ii. wheat   iii. streets

2. **a** In an alley paved with trash, a flower grows.
   b It stands alone, an upturned bell.
   a How did it get there? The cruel wind knows,
   b A secret the wind will never_____.

   i. knows   ii. stirs   iii. tell

3. **a** A shower of tears rains down on the stone.
   a This mountain and I are both soaked to the_____.

   i. clothes   ii. bone   iii. skin

You're the author! Write your own couplet with an a/a/b/b pattern.

cinquains   Name _____

Two Crazy Cats

Poetry tells about feelings, ideas, or events, often with fewer words than regular writing. A **cinquain** is a five-line poem that does not rhyme. The different parts of speech are used to make up a cinquain.

grass	Line 1: a noun
fresh, green	Line 2: two adjectives describing the noun
blowing, whispering, touching	Line 3: three verbs ending in "ing"
tickles between my toes	Line 4: tells something about the noun
meadow	Line 5: another noun like the one in Line 1

Use the list to complete the poems about the two cats, Samantha and Stripes. Write the correct word or phrase on each line.

Word and Phrase List

sleeping, purring, eating   watching with eyes wide open   lazy, fat   kitten
   toy for a cat   dark, quiet   prowling, pouncing, playing   yarn

1. cat
   _____
   _____
   likes to lie on things
   Samantha

2. _____
   soft, yellow
   rolling, unwinding, tangling
   _____
   string

3. _____
   slim, graceful
   climbing, jumping, running
   _____
   Stripes

4. night
   _____
   _____
   fun for two crazy cats
   playtime

You're the author! Write a cinquain about your favorite animal.

Published by Instructional Fair. Copyright protected.   IF87134 *Building Writing Skills*

limericks

Name _____

Loony Limericks

A **limerick** is a silly five-line poem with rhyming lines. The first, second, and fifth lines rhyme and have three beats. The third and fourth lines rhyme and have two beats. A beat is a syllable that has a strong stress when you say it.

line 1	a	While eating a fresh apple **pie**,
line 2	a	Ed heard the soft buzz of a **fly**.
line 3	b	He swatted the **air**,
line 4	b	But nothing was **there**;
line 5	a	The fly had buzzed off to the **sky**!

Circle the best lines to finish these limericks.

1. When asked if his dog would bite,

   The man said, "Try him, he might."

   But when I turned my head,

   The *man* bit me instead!

   a. His dog laughed as I ran out of sight.

   b. And the paper he wrote on was white.

2. There once was a hungry old snake

   Who swallowed his tail by mistake.

   As he gobbled it down,

   He gave a big frown,

   a. And he ran to the doctor in town.

   b. And he said, "I would rather eat cake."

You're the author! Write your own limerick using the **a/a/b/b/a** pattern.

Answer Key

Under the Sea (identifying complete sentences) 4
1. purple
2. green
3. purple
4. green
5. purple
6. green
7. purple

Itty Bitty Bugs (identifying types of sentences) 5
1. question
2. statement
3. statement
4. command
5. exclamation
6. question
7. statement
8. exclamation
9. command
10. statement

The Hike (capitals and end marks) 6
1. This trail is rocky and steep.
2. I almost fell! or, I almost fell.
3. Juan wants to see some deer.
4. Did we bring water to drink?
5. Pick up that trash. or, Pick up that trash!
6. Who saw that hawk fly over the field?

A Trip to the Zoo (identifying complete sentences) 7
1. S
2. S
3. F
4. S
5. F
6. S
7. S
8. F
9. F
10. S

Sentences made from 3, 5, 8, or 9 will vary.

It's a Puzzle! (word order) 8
1. I have a jigsaw puzzle.
2. It has a hundred pieces.
3. John and Oscar help me.
4. This puzzle is fun!
5. Ahmed works a crossword puzzle.
6. He stops to help us.
7. Iko builds a wooden puzzle.
8. We all have a great time.

Peanut Butter and Jelly (subjects/predicates) 9
1. My mom makes lunch for me.
2. Grape jelly is made from grapes and sugar.
3. Peanut butter sticks to the roof of my mouth.
4. Milk is good to drink with my sandwich.
5. I am eating lunch.
6. Chips and cookies are on my plate, too.
7. All my friends like my sandwiches the best.
8. Lunch is my favorite meal!

The Toy Store (subjects) 10
1. The toy boat
2. I
3. The doll with the black hair
4. Tiny cars
5. She
6. The stuffed elephant
7. Marbles
8. That board game

Additional sentences will vary.

Toys, Toys, Toys (predicates) 11
1. has real lights!
2. can drive over rocks and mud.
3. loves toy horses.
4. is the fastest.
5. makes a great gift.
6. have a model plane.
7. are fun.
8. beeps loudly.

Additional sentences will vary.

Once Upon a Time (subjects and predicates) 12
1. (Cinderella) worked hard.
2. (Lon Po Po) is a scary wolf.
3. (The Blue Fairy) turned Pinnochio into a real boy!
4. (The Three Little Pigs) had wolf stew.
5. (Sleeping Beauty) slept for a hundred years.
6. (Snow White and Sleepy) were friends.
7. (The Three Billy Goats Gruff) fooled the troll.
8. (Goldilocks) slept in the little bear's bed.
9. (Anansi) is a tricky spider.
10. (Jack) climbed the beanstalk.
11. (Beast) fell in love with Beauty.
12. (Fairy tales) are good stories.

Wild Wolves (subjects and predicates) 13
1. (Wolves) have thick fur to keep them warm.
2. (Dogs) are related to wolves.
3. (A den) is a hole in the ground where wolves live.
4. (Wolves) eat meat.
5. (Wolves) hunt together in a pack.
6. (Wolf pups) play outside when they are three to four weeks old.
7. (The alpha wolf) is the strongest wolf in the pack.
8. (A snarling wolf) is angry.
9. (Wolves) can see well in the dark.
10. (Some wolves) live in the United States.
11. (Many stories) have a big, bad wolf.
12. (Wolves) are not really bad animals.

The Fire (nouns and pronouns) 14
1. The brave firefighters—firefighters
2. A loud bell—bell
3. They—They
4. One person—person
5. The siren—siren
6. We—We
7. A spotted dog—dog
8. It—It
9. Thick, black smoke—smoke

Answer Key

10. Some firefighters—firefighters
11. They—They
12. The firefighters—firefighters
13. They—They
14. Everyone—Everyone
15. The fire truck—truck

Lights, Camera, Action! (action verbs) 15
1. dances
2. runs
3. sleeps
4. jumps
5. swings

Quiet, Please! (nonaction verbs) 16
1. is
2. were
3. are
4. has
5. had
6. have
7. is
8. has
9. am
10. has
11. are
12. is

How Does Your Garden Grow?
(present-tense subject/verb agreement) 17
1. like
2. tastes
3. eat
4. scares
5. crawls
6. moves
7. grow
8. plants
9. waters
10. begin
11. enjoy
12. want

Going Up! (present tense—to be) 18
1. are
2. am
3. are
4. are
5. are
6. is
7. is
8. is
9. is
10. is
11. is
12. am
13. is
14. are

Ed, Ted, and Fred (past-tense regular verbs) 19
walked, wanted, remembered, used, waited, started, enjoyed, watched, played

Look Before You Leap (past-tense irregular verbs) ..20
1. came
2. ate
3. saw
4. said
5. ran
6. fell
7. gave
8. made
9. went

Monkey Business (past tense—to be) 21
1. were
2. was
3. were
4. were
5. were
6. was
7. was
8. was
9. was
10. were
11. was
12. were
13. was
14. were
15. were
16. were

The Turtle's Trip
(past-tense subject/verb agreement) 22
wanted, knew, belonged, went, shared, was, helped, loved, came, walked, saw, hid, smiled

This and That (compound subjects) 23
1. Girls and boys play baseball.
2. Penguins and seals walk on snow.
3. Red roses and yellow tulips grow in the garden.
4. Ribbons and bows make a gift look pretty.

Read and Write (compound predicates) 24
1. Kayla runs and plays.
2. Wu adds and subtracts numbers.
3. Marena looks at a map and finds her hometown.
4. Nakita goes to the library and checks out books.

A Birthday Party (compound sentences) 25
candles 1, 4, 5, 6, and 8 should be colored
1. , and
4. , but
5. , and
6. , or
8. , and

A Winter's Day (compound sentences) 26
1. , and
2. , or
3. , but
4. Juan makes a snow angel, and Anita makes snowballs.
5. Anita throws a snowball, but Juan just laughs.
6. Answers will vary

The Best Day Ever! (run-on sentences) 27
1. I hopped out of bed. The sun was shining.
2. My mom fixed pancakes. I didn't have to go to school.
3. My dad wanted to go on a safari. I wanted to go, too.
4. We rode across the plains. I saw lions and elephants.
5. We stopped for dinner, and we ate zebra pie.
6. My mom tucked me into bed, and my dad read me a story.

All Tied Up (stringy sentences) 28
packages with string: 1, 4, 5

Answer Key

Eli Is Excited! (stringy sentences) 29
1. I will make the best game in the world. Everyone will play. I will be the star. My friends will play, too.

2. I think the moon is made of cheese. We can send people to the moon, and they can eat. Then, no one has to be hungry.

Packing a Suitcase (commas in a series) 30
1. We are going on a trip to Japan, China, and Korea.
2. My mother, father, sister, and I are packing our suitcases.
3. I need to pack my soap, toothbrush, and comb.
4. Mom, I can't find my socks, shoes, or underwear!
5. I can take my blue jeans, green shorts, and purple socks.
6. Do I need tennis shoes, nice shoes, or sandals?
7. A wallet, a book, and a watch are also good things to pack.
8. Should I pack a book, a game, or a yo-yo?
9. The tickets, bags, and maps are all ready.
10. Mom tucks me in, kisses me, and tells me good night.
11. Mom turns out the lights in my room, the hall, and the stairs.
12. I can't wait to travel, play, and have fun!

Adjective Art (adding adjectives) 31
1. two   4. apple   7. Three
2. blue   5. yellow   8. red
3. four   6. puffy   9. pretty

Oh, Say, Can You See? (adding adjectives) 32
1. red, blue
2. fifty, thirteen
3. courage
4. six
5. stars
6. Flag
7. Old
8. Star-Spangled

The Case of the Missing Grapes (how and when) .. 33
1. When did Caleb take a nap?
2. When did Mr. Smith wash his hands?
3. How hungry was Kelly?
4. When did Sven go to work?
5. When did Kelly read? or, How long did Kelly read?
6. When did Sam put the grapes away?
7. How did Martha eat her lunch?
8. Mr. Smith took the missing grapes.

Hide and Seek (where) 34
1. in   6. above
2. under   7. outside
3. behind   8. along
4. next
5. on

Save the Day (vivid verbs) 35
1. zoomed   6. burned
2. strapped   7. rescued
3. cried   8. pulled
4. streaked   9. thundered
5. roared   10. shouted

Just Because (cause and effect) 36
1. b.   5. e.   9. k.
2. d.   6. h.   10. i.
3. a.   7. g.   11. l.
4. c.   8. f.   12. j.

Super Sentences! (the 5Ws + how) 37
1. A tiny toad hopped quickly under the porch to hide when the rain started.
2. The shiny rocket blasted loudly into the air this morning to go to Mars.
3. The elves quietly fixed the cobbler's shoes in his shop to help him while he was sleeping.

Under Construction (building sentences) 38
1. The tall man strolls slowly through the store looking for a new clock.
2. The kitten purred softly in the den while sitting on Mom's lap.
3. A car raced by our house with three dogs chasing it late last night.

The order of phrases may vary.

Ready, Set, Morph! (complex sentences) 39
1. When it gets warm, ice melts.
2. At school, we have to behave.
3. At the start of the summer, we go to the cottage.
4. Outside his spaceship, the alien turned into a bug.
5. After it rains, sometimes a rainbow comes out.
6. With time, kittens grow into cats.

What's the Big Idea? (paragraphs) 40
1. People wear many different things on their feet. keys
2. Bugs are everywhere. snow
3. I love to paint. eggs

Field Day (extraneous details) 41
Cross out:
I eat eggs and toast for breakfast.
I like to play a computer racing game at home.
My teacher is very nice.

Answer Key

Our school was built in 1989.
Mr. Lee is the history teacher.

Animal Addresses (indentation) 42
X before "Other mice live in fields."
X before "Jungles all over the world are in danger."

Topics in the Tropics (topic sentences) 43
Parrots are beautiful birds that live in the tropics.
My family is having a luau.
Hawaii is an interesting place.

Up, Up, and Away (topic sentences) 44
1. b.
2. a.
3. Answers will vary, but should include "things you need to know to fly a balloon."

Lean on a Friend (supporting sentences) 45
1. topic   4. topic
2. supporting 5. supporting
3. supporting 6. supporting
Supporting sentences will vary.

Perfect Pizza (examples) 46
   Pizza is my favorite food for three reasons. First, it is hot and bubbly. The cheese is melted, and steam rises from the pizza. Second, the toppings are great! My favorites are pepperoni and black olives. Third, pizza is easy to share. Pizza comes eight slices to a box. Pick up a slice, and you're ready to eat. I think pizza is perfect!
Additional examples will vary.

Build a Bridge (transitions) 47
Golden Gate Bridge paragraph: First, Second, Then, Finally
Bridges paragraph: One, Another, Often, Today

In the Kitchen (sequencing) 48
Lemonade: 3, 1, 2
Peanut-butter squares: 2, 1, 3, 4, 6, 7, 5

Great Endings (concluding sentences) 49
1. You will love this book.
2. What a thrilling book!
3. Wouldn't you like to go on an adventure with Jack and Annie?

End of the Day (concluding sentences) 50
1. b.
2. b.
3. Answers will vary.

Horsing Around (expository paragraphs) 51
1. First, they are beautiful animals.
   Second, I love to ride horses.
   Third, horses are very smart.
2. a. They have bright eyes and shiny coats.
   b. I like to gallop in the woods.
   c. They understand all kinds of commands.

Sssssssssnakes! (informative paragraphs) 52
Cross out:
   Kenny has two snakes.
   The snake at the zoo is named Monty.
   I like snakes.
The remaining sentences should be written in logical order.

Stripes or Spots? (descriptive paragraphs) 53
type: garter snake   size: small
color: black   pattern: stripes
garter snake, small, black, stripes

How Do You Do It? (how-to paragraphs) 54
First, you need a glass cage, a heat lamp, food, and some water.

Then, set up the cage with a small bowl of water and a heat lamp.

Also, when you touch a snake, always pet it from head to tail.

Finally, different kinds of snakes eat different kinds of food.

Why? Oh, Why? (cause-and-effect paragraphs) 55
1. b.
2. c.
3. a.

I have to watch my snake, Jake, more closely. Yesterday, I took him out of his cage to clean it. (He got away when I was not looking.) He slithered as fast as lightning into the kitchen. (My mom screamed loudly and jumped on a chair.) Jake hid under the stove. (I looked for a long time before I found him.) Now he is back in his cage. Next time, I plan to put him in a box while I clean his cage!
Answers may vary slightly.

**Snakes or Dogs
(compare-and-contrast paragraphs)** 56
Snake: eats as needed
       needs a heat lamp
       no training classes
Dog: needs training classes
       eats every day
       needs to go for walks
Same: both are pets

Published by Instructional Fair. Copyright protected.   IF87134 Building Writing Skills

Answer Key

both need care
both are fun
Compare and contrast: eats, walks, heat

PLEASE!! (persuasive paragraphs) 57
1. for
2. for
3. against
4. against
5. for
6. for
7. against
8. for

Paragraphs will vary, but should have "for" reasons.

Happy Birthday! (identifying expository paragraphs) 58
1. persuasive
2. how-to
3. compare-and-contrast
4. descriptive
5. cause-and-effect
6. informative

Sweet Seasons (multiple paragraphs) 60
underlined topic sentences:
   My two favorite seasons are winter and spring.
   Winter is fun, but spring is beautiful!
   Even though summer means no school, it's my least favorite season.
   It's great to relax, but summer is usually too hot and humid.
circled concluding sentence:
   I'll take winter and spring over summer any day!

The Truth About Homework (five-paragraph essays) 61
1. a.
2. b.
3. c.
4. d.
5. e.

Whale Tails and Whale Tales (recognizing stories) 62
1. narrative
2. expository
3. narrative

Murray's Mix-up (beginning, middle, end) 63
1. beginning
2. end
3. middle
4. end
5. middle
6. beginning
7. end

Where in the World? (settings) 64
1. a.
2. b.
3. b.
4. b.
5. in the kitchen
6. at night

Who's Who? (characters) 65
1. d.
2. a.
3. c.
4. e.
5. b.

Who Said That? (characters) 66
1. he remembers the day each of us was born.
2. they could get hurt if they run in the halls.
3. this was not his lucky day.
4. she wouldn't do well, even though she studied.
5. there was never a more beautiful sight.

What's the Problem? (problems) 67
1. c.
2. b.
3. a.

Try, Try Again (events) 68
1. a.
2. b.

Final Reports (solutions) 69
1. event, event, solution
2. 3, 1, 2

One Small Light (story structure) 71
1. when: October
   where: by the sea
2. Chen and Lee (brother and sister)
3. Lee couldn't see her brother's boat and didn't know if he was safe.
4. First, she tried to light her lamp.
5. Next, she tried blowing her whistle.
6. Then, she called her brother's name.
7. Finally, she saw a light on the water and heard her brother's voice. She knew he was safe.

Answers may vary slightly.

Look at It This Way (point of view) 72
1. first person; He (She) crawled slowly down into the dark hole.
2. narrator; I jumped from one tree to the next like a squirrel.
3. first person; He (She) never wanted to see another bug in his (her) life!
4. narrator; I wrote quickly, trying to finish before the buzzer.
5. narrator; I play the game better than anyone.

Answer Key

A Million Questions (leads/hooks) 73
1. a.
2. b.
3. a.
4. a.
5. Answers will vary.

Mrs. Reid's Vase (story transitions) 74
Mrs. Reid's favorite vase was broken last night at dinner. Before dinner, Janet picked up the vase to look at it. While they were eating, Miguel tapped his fork against it to see if it was glass. Suddenly, lightning flashed outside, and the room went black. While it was dark, Khalil heard a cat screech and jump onto the table. When the lights came back on, the vase was broken.

The County Fair (descriptions) 75
1. green
2. red
3. blue
4. red
5. orange
6. yellow
7. blue
8. green
9. orange

What the Reader Sees (show, don't tell) 76
1. c.
2. b.
3. a.
4. c.
5. b.
Last sentence will vary.

Show and Tell (action) 77
1. showing
2. telling
3. showing
4. Paragraphs will vary.

What's That, You Say? (dialogue) 78
"Where are you going?" asked Ben.
"I'm going to Luke's party," replied Wauneka.
"Hey! Let's ride together," said Ben.

"Whooo's there?" called Uncle Hoot in his deep voice.
She said, "Hello, Uncle Hoot. It's me, Milly."
"Who? Who?" asked Uncle Hoot.

Snow Day! (quotation marks) 79
1. "You may play after you get dressed," said Mom.
2. Marco hollered from his room, "Has anyone seen my gloves?"
3. "Look under your bed," said Mom, "or maybe in the closet."
4. "Are you going to build a snowman today?" asked Dad.
5. Maya exclaimed, "Let's go! I'm ready!"
6. "You may go," said Mom, "when Marco is ready."
7. "Hey!" said Maya. "Don't throw snowballs at me."
8. "Did Marco throw it?" asked Dad.
9. "It wasn't me! Mom did it," laughed Marco.
Answers may vary slightly.

The Grand Wedding (indenting quotes) 80
The knight shouted, "Listen, everyone! My friend's son is to be married."
"When is the day?" shouted the baker.
"A week after we bring in the harvest. The whole town is invited!" said the farmer
"Hurray for the good farmer!" cheered the crowd.

Fantastic Finishes (endings) 81
1. a.
2. b.

It's All in the Name (story titles) 82
1. c.
2. <u>Sarah, Plain and Tall</u>
3. <u>Stone Fox</u>
4. <u>The Relatives Came</u>
5. <u>Number the Stars</u>
6. <u>A Light in the Attic</u>

Tell Me a Story (story elements) 83
Across:
4. events
8. transitions
11. characters
12. beginning
13. end

Down:
1. setting
2. lead
3. point of view
5. title
6. problem
7. middle
9. solution
10. dialogue

Crash! Bang! Boom! (onomatopoeia) 84
1. e.
2. b.
3. f.
4. h.
5. d.
6. c.
7. a.

Answer Key

8. g.
9. i.
10. j.

**Silly Safari Animals
(alliteration and assonance) 85**
1. alliteration
   l sounds circled
2. alliteration
   z sounds circled
3. assonance
   o sounds circled
4. assonance
   e sounds circled
5. alliteration
   g sounds circled
6. assonance
   o sounds circled
7. assonance
   u sounds circled
8. alliteration
   j sounds circled (or, assonance, u sounds)
9. alliteration
   f sounds circled (or, assonance, i sounds)
10. alliteration
    w sounds circled

Just Like That (similes) 86
1. quiet   7. sank
2. hot   8. cold
3. quick   9. sing
4. runs
5. stubborn
6. grown
Additional sentences will vary.

The Angry River (personification) 87
1. teased
2. angry, beat, shouted
3. roaring, frightened, lonely
4. stood, tossed
5. sad, swam
6. bit
7. groaned with pain
8. grew tired, went to sleep
9. lay back down
10. limped, hugged
Additional answers will vary.

What Shall I Write? (choosing a topic) 88
1. b.
2. a.
3. a.
4. b.
5. a.
Additional answers will vary.

Prompt Me (prompts) 89
1. narrative
2. expository
3. expository
4. narrative
5. expository
6. expository
7. expository
8. narrative

What a Plan! (planning expository writing) 90
1. c.
2a. a.
 b. f.
3a. g.
 b. b.
4a. d.
 b. e.
5. h.

My Dream Truck (description planning) 91
2a. deep metallic blue
 b. silver stripes
3a. chrome wheels
 b. huge tires
4a. cool stereo
 b. Answers should relate to a car stereo.
Answers for vacation may be in any order, but should display three distinct details.

A Treasure Map (narrative planning) 92
1a. e.   3. c.
 b. d.   4. f.
 c. a.   5. b.
2. g.

The Moon (staying on topic) 93
Rocks on the Moon: cross out the second paragraph and "I wonder what the astronauts drank."
A Race to the Moon: cross out "I wonder what it was like to watch that race." "The moon is very old." and "My dad watched it on TV."

Is That Your Mummy? (extraneous information) 94
1. in pyramids or in Egypt
2. Also or too
3. from Egypt
4. and from a long time ago
5. Mummies were buried with treasure. or, Mummies were buried with gold, gems, and jewels.
6. Gold workers made beautiful art. After 3,000 years, the figs are too hard to eat now. I like reading about mummies.

A New Planet (elaboration) 95
1. a.   3. b.
2. b.   4. b.

Published by Instructional Fair. Copyright protected.   IF87134 Building Writing Skills

Answer Key

That's Clear (specific writing) 96
1. b.   3. b.
2. b.   4. a.

Swamp Water (unclear references) 97
1. Maria
2. tree
3. One Fang or, a big alligator
4. Maria
5. Jacques
6. he: the swamp rat

Sentence will vary.

Vesuvius (revising fragments) 98
fragments:
   A very famous volcano.
   The market city, Pompeii.
   Like the time it buried Pompeii.
   Because the volcano is still so dangerous.
Rewritten sentences will vary.

Too Many Little Ones (varying sentences) 99
1. There are more than twenty elves in my uncle's attic.
2. The elves make a lot of noise when they stay up all night.
3. Elves play in the kitchen and the music room.

Answers may vary slightly.
Paragraphs will vary.

Fishing with my Grandfather (editing verbs) 100
1. a.   5. b.
2. b.   6. c.
3. c.   7. a.
4. b.   8. a.

Apples for Everyone (editing spelling) 101
1. famile—family
2. bigest—biggest
3. peece—piece
4. are—our
5. freinds—friends
6. happend—happened
7. threw—through
8. Thay—They
9. hole—whole
10. runing—running

The Great Horse Escape (editing punctuation) 102
1. a.
2. c.
3. b.
4. c.
5. a.

Awful Ads (editing capitalization) 103
1. These, One, I
2. *Treasure Island*, *The Lorax*, Come, Book, Kahn, There, Booker's, At
3. The Auto Place, Now, *Amazing Automobiles*

Messy Monsters (editing paragraphing) 104
Paragraph notations before:
   The next night, Rose left a plate of cookies in the middle of the room.
   "Write a note to remind yourself to clean up your room," said her mother.
   "The mess is in your room," said her mom, "so you have to clean it up."

Favorite Fairy Tales (short answers) 105
1. Goldilocks visited the Three Bear's house.
2. Little Red Riding Hood was going to visit her grandmother.
3. The Big Bad Wolf tried to blow down the houses of the Three Little Pigs.
4. Cinderella wore glass slippers.
5. Beast fell in love with Beauty.
6. Cinderella left the ball at midnight.
7. Pinocchio's nose grew when he lied.
8. Most fairy tales end happily ever after.

Answers may vary slightly.

The Odd Octopus (short answers) 106
1. b.
2. c.

What's the Point? (summaries) 107
1. b.
2. a.

The Lost City (summaries) 108
1. c.
2. Answers will vary.

Mean Sam Clemm (book reports) 109
1. a grumpy cowboy and a child.
2. leaves his horse by the bank.
3. looks at his horse.
4. the little girl shows Sam a smiley-face pattern on the horse.
5. Answer will vary.

All answers will vary in wording.

Take Note of This (taking notes) 110
1. c.
2. c.

Geysers of Yellowstone (taking notes) 111
1. Yellowstone has many geysers.
2. melted rock heats water
3. boiling water erupts
4. Old Faithful is well known.

Answer Key

    5. it erupts on time
    6. water shoots 184 feet (56m) in the air

Harriet Tubman (summarizing) 112
    c.

The Exxon *Valdez* (summarizing) 113
    c.

Dear Grandma (friendly letters) 114
    1. signature
    2. heading
    3. closing
    4. body
    5. greeting
    6. heading, closing, signature

An Invitation (friendly letters) 115
    1. October 12, 1492
    2. Sincerely,
    3. My dear Mr. Claus,
    4. Yours very truly,

                      March 15, 2002
Dear Jeremy,
I wish you could play basketball on our team. We start practice on April 3. Can you join us? I hope so!
                      Your friend,
                      Olivia

It's in the Mail (addressing envelopes) 116
    1. Mrs. Harriet Colles
       845 Pine Street
       Garnet, Montana 59770

    2. Shelby Perkins
       3572 Sunshine Lane
       Davies, Florida 32802

    3. Return addresses will vary.

    Nathaniel Apayauk
    72 Tundra Road
    Barrow, Alaska 99723

A Couple of Couplets (poetry) 117
    1. ii.
    2. iii.
    3. ii.

Two Crazy Cats (cinquains) 118
    1. lazy, fat; sleeping, purring, eating
    2. yarn; toy for a cat
    3. kitten; watching with eyes wide open
    4. dark, quiet; prowling, pouncing, playing

Loony Limericks (limericks) 119
    1. a.
    2. b.
    3. Answers will vary.